In the
Terrified
Radiance

IN THE
TERRIFIED
RADIANCE

A book of new poems by
STANLEY BURNSHAW
with selections from his
earlier volumes

GEORGE BRAZILLER
New York

ACKNOWLEDGMENTS
The author records his thanks to Holt, Rinehart and
Winston, Inc. for enabling him to include in this volume
selections from his *Caged in an Animal's Mind* published
by Holt, Rinehart and Winston, Inc.
For other acknowledgments, see pp. 205 *ff., passim.*

First printing
Standard Book Number: 0-8076-0652-9, cloth
Standard Book Number: 0-8076-0653-7, paper
Library of Congress Catalogue Card Number: 72-80013
Printed in the United States of America

I · The Terrified Radiance

II · Women and Men

v

FROM *Caged in an Animal's Mind (1963)*

vii

FROM *Early and Late Testament (1952)*

FROM *The Iron Land (1936)*

ix

In the
Terrified
Radiance

I

The Terrified Radiance

To a Crow

In the sea above where the crests
Of pine make a ring on the sky,
Watching your fires prepare
Their killer-dive to the ground,

I think of the closed-in ocean
That presses against the shore
Its striving lives unwatched
Or known, and among the known

Your counterself in the sea:
Darkness of water's fire,
The driver against all walls
And tides, yet fatefully borne

On its self-devouring will
To breed.   So can it seem
To a creature living on land
Who watches above and below

As he walks the middleground
In search of clues that his body
Lost.   He may even ask
If to kill is your sign from the air,

To kill and then consume;
If your other sign from the sea
Is to breed and slowly die,
Though you are not quite bird

Nor fish but mortal kindred

Spreading through water and wind
Your signs more false than true
For one who can neither swim

Nor fly but, hovering, makes
The dying live, and strives
To tell with his skin and eyes
The differing selves of darkness —

Darkness of fish from bird's,
Color of night from death —

Innocent War

(*Gloss: lines 29-30, "To a Crow"*)

"To make the dying live" —

Somber name for the will
At the root of human love,

The one wild gift that men
Could add to the world's landscape,

Staying the spill of blood
From falling body and leaf:

Learn from the innocent war
Against the pull of the lifeless?

Gulls . . .

Gulls
Drop their unreachable prey from the air
Till the shells
Crack on the dying stone open

        I hear
Windows opened by trees — I hear
Seeds, the sunfire,
Rain soothing and flailing,
Sandfloors pushing up from the sea —

Tomorrow — yesterday — now:
Silence:noise — I hear them
Everywhere, anywhere . . .

    Days burn out and nights
    Boil into dawns —

Under the hiding wave
Prey calm in their guardian shells live,
Wait, while the gulls seize,
Pound through unbreakable air
The stone that wears its life away into sand.

Central Park: Midwinter

When you cross the path toward the meadow,
Ponder a speckled snow,
But do not look for the blankness
That crushes country hills
To a faith of animal peace
White in a more than white.
Watch for onyx, the dust
Of grayblue flakes in a wind
Of smoldering jewels poured down
From mouths of the lower sky
At the crests of our stone towers.

And if you forget this ash
Was grown on ancestral trees
Of sun, torn from their depths
Of mineral peace to yield
Slumbering fire, you will see them
Gasping up toward the height
But sinking down through air
To shed their final leaves
Into their kindred trees.
Watch them write on the snow
Their hieroglyphs of passage,

And believe that none who were here
Before us thirsted beyond
Their worlds of green ascent
Or turned from the sight of blooming
Trees to thoughts of a deathly
Wood in the crushed prairies

Of blackness. Only a creature
Starved for warmth would think
To make out of coal tombs
A second coming of sun
Before the passionless ash.

The Finding Light

Suddenly at my feet
A small rock breaks apart at a vein:

Openness always dying, without the shield of a skin —
More bruisable naked than else on earth is stone:

The tenderness ever surrounding, ever unseen,
Ever in wait

For the finding light its strife wrings from a man.

Erstwhile Hunter

Savaging land, the killer gale
Blown by the life from nowhere finally
Reels against the indestructible
     Sea.   He will shear the crippled
Trees, he will bring the scalded stalks
     And boughs the single grace

He owns: expunge caprice with fire,
That leaf and blood once again regrow
Veils of calm and dare to nourish,
     Breathe, to sleep with quiet
Eyes under an ever prowling
     Heaven. — Who of the spared

But this broken self could scorn and exalt
The need that will make him torture his thought
On the lost? who but the erstwhile hunter
     Become a nurse to flowers
More scourges ago than hands could ever
     Uncover of axes abandoned

By the sleeping caves of the world.

Their Singing River

Sometimes, dazed in a field, I think I hear
Voices rocking the trees; then I stop, race
To the boughs, listen — and hear not even a thread
Of a wind.

        The calling voices never resound
In aftertones that would make your ears believe,
Nor is there other proof except my temples'
Shaken emptiness. Nor can I know, if my body
Had leaped to the tree in time, what they might have said,
What I might have answered. Or if some other signs
Could show their presence.

          Now I cannot regain
Even by wilful dreaming the father faces
Or the eye or hair of the ancient women who bore me
Or think to imagine how they might pull me now
Into the redness of their singing river.

Not To Bereave . . .

Not to bereave is to praise the bridled
Rays that keep each body rising
    Or falling. Who can be taken
That has not called with a sign to the seizer
    "Come, I am here."

Slaking caresses blind the blood:
Few die but have felt the scorching
    Bliss of a killer's desire
In a closed house or under the chained
    Sky where an otter

Sinks to the sea's floor to gather
A stone that will break the clam he holds
    Close to his breast. While the flint
Will of the earth suffuses: forces
    All it contains,

What will you teach your veins? The bird
Trapped from birth in a cell hidden
    From any sound, on the dawn
Inscribed in his blood, bursts with the same
    Cry that his brother

Shouts from the wood. Tangled in skeins
Of will and knowledge, how can you know
    Sight as desire, who dare not

Glance at the furies that crush your sun?
    Shielding your eyes,

While the flint will of the earth suffuses:
Forces all it contains to thrive,
    Wings cry up from the dark
Singing as the clam dies in the song
    Of the preying stone.

(For James Dickey)

Underbreathing Song

Men have daytime eyes.
Nobody goes to the woods at night
To work the trees.   Even your skin
Knows when the light dies
To a blindness on its covering.   Sight
Lifts and falls with the sun,

But voices neither wake
Nor sleep in cells of bone and flesh:
They live you and re-live, they speak
In underbreathing song.
What if you cannot say the words
Of their dark-and-daylight tongue:

Its murmurs are your wave
Tying you to your turning sphere
Too vast to behold, too wild to distill
Calm until you believe
Certainties flow from unwilled voices
That never reach your ear.

Emptiness . . .

Emptiness seeps through the air, it is seeping
Into our clothes.   Where it blows from nobody
Knows, yet the dangling tie clinches
The neck, the shoulders chafe.   It could come,
We knew, the Unthinkable, but this cannot be
The one we saw.   Shelters abound:
Nobody tries the doors.   Everyone
Seems to be standing-listening as though
Expecting shrieks of a rain from a possible
Further sky.

       Is it still too soon
To wonder what if the fume could burn
Through all this skin?   The light widens.
Some have begun to tear their clothes
Without waiting to ask.   To learn, we were told,
Is to wait and ask — nothing was said of a presence.

Arms

If arms go weak at the thought of flight,
What will you do when a final dark
Deepens — trust that your skin will trace
Glimmers of useable light?

And if it fail, when you have no choice,
You and your children, before you fall
But to roam an unknown eyeless land
Where your voice will be your only hand

For reaching — can you stay cold to the call
Of your arms or will an embittered spark
Of their holy trust again devour
The unforeseeable flower?

Procreations

. . . and yet and everywhere
Wreaths are curling up from the sand:
The sea's salt with the leaf's land
        In a fuse of air:
Bursts of streaming shape and sound,
Twining creations of soil and mist —

        Watching near and far
To draw from the ever-unfolding swarm
        Sparks of bestowing form,
And failing at our own command,
We weary towers out of a cave,
Forcing upon the inviolate ground
        Our witness stones . . .

        And will this need desist
        When coming nothing stands,
When the rock rises against the wave
        With taking hands?

The Terrified Radiance

Because there is no forever
And any bird has as much to hope for
As any man, I can look on all I have made
With coldness, with relief —

Gather the scraps and sketches,
Bundle them into somber heaps,
Hide them in closets against the ever possible
Moment of need

For trading them one by one
To a friendless hearth where perhaps their ashen
Bodies may fan a second fire with the lucky
Loveable traces

That once had forced my fingers
Holding the pen to raise up visions
They had not known.   Because there is no forever
For any being,

I want no portal hollowed
Out of the equal selves of soil,
Grass, or stone to guard my breathless heap
That must one day burden

A room, a field.   For I know
And wish that whatever I am, after
A season, will die from the minds of those I leave
As those I loved

Have died from mine, mother,
Father, friends of the hearth, all —
All but a cold company of strangers distant
In time and country,

Violent ones whose thoughts
Have been burning coals in my veins and keeping
My heart from falling into the lost disease
Of numbness to this eden,

That flows from the terrified radiance of our minds.

II

Women and Men

Movie Poster on a Subway Wall

Whenever I pass her — morning, evening —
Her motionless sight sends visions trembling
Beyond enravishment, threads of my brain
Brushing against her hair, her mouth,
Her body's roses, till other threads
Signal remembrance and leave me only
Her tomb in a paper image —

                              I think
Of withered Donne on his sickbed tossed
In his clouds of angel lightning, begging
The gaze of his gods: I remember his cry
To the wonder of flesh that is earth, the wildness
Of hair that is grown out of earth, the reaches
Of mind,

              till my shaking eyes have lost
All strength to scour the streets for a sight
That might reconcile the image and tomb
Of loves that would live in me yet die.

End of a Visit

"I am going back — now," I say and you nod
Half-sorrowing, half-smiling.
We both look at the clock.

'I'll write, of course — next week perhaps' — a bird
Grazes a screen; startled,
Flies upward, darts down.

                    I gather
My parcels, books, coat; glance at your face
          (It is time to go from a child,
A woman now, bruised; with a place for her head,
          thought, and arms, and a trail
Her body reads in the dark)

                              "I must go back."

                              'I know — it's time.'

Drawn to the door, I hold it,
Open it, speak, half-aware
That while I repeat my words
The dim roundness to which we cling will be fleeing
Another countless thousand miles from nowhere to nowhere.

San Francisco, 1966

34

The Echoing Shape

What can you do alone all day?

Look for the cloud in the sun — listen
For underseas in the air — follow
A leaf, a weed . . .

At night?

I try
To take the darkness.   Nothing of shape outside begins
To speak to me: their daylight
Burns my ears: I gather in midnight waves.
My cat watches at my feet, both of us
Hoping to know what she hears in the blackness rolling
From across the lake where a bird
Sings for its branches.   How can I know
That the bird is blind?   It may not be there when dawn comes
And though I could creep up close, in another silence,
I would be watching as always with eyes that recover
From whatever can kindle their light
An echoing shape of arms, thighs, shoulders — the severed
Shadows of all the visions they have ever loved.

Summer Morning Train to the City

Not you closed in a self,
Not even the skin of your fingers damp to the
      morning paper
Looking at me with their hundred eyes,
Or the perfume
Swarming out of their crevices,
Nor even the pink bulge in bracelets of heat
Of your knees giving out signals . . .

And my right hand stirs in anonymous will to go
      streaming
Over the fields that lie near your hidden country's
Imagined hills of flesh, to gentle apart
The twinning legs as it enters
The thighs' bounds, to learn the warmth and upward
To the heavier breath as it moves into where the fruit
Might rouse to the hundred tips of fire, vibrating
Fingers of kiss, scar, squeeze, and release
Till the swollen pear scream to be pierced and bitten.

— Legs uncross.   The eyes of your self glance beyond the
      paper
Past my eyes toward the train window and through to the
      yards,
Unaware of our bond.   O trainmate, look at the chained
      hand
Of the morning rite's oblation!

The captive we see is heavy,
Swollen still with the blood of its stopped-up wanting:
      Where can it go,

Summoned here minutes ago by a need beginning and ending
        its sudden autonymous life
In a body searching for passageways toward a timeless
        world?
Not you, not I, but a hand
And a fruit drawing the hand that has only to breach a
        covering —
Let us watch together the fire draining back to its
        hungering nowhere.

Women and Men

Women and men who have long
Lived together will die
Together however distant
The nights of their separate going:

If more than bodies entwine
In the suddenly swelling roses
Of skin, will more than their arms
Cling for the fusing dew?

Across the estranging waters
That wind about their years
Thoughts-not-words ceaselessly
Wander from blood to blood,

One toward the other, of eyes,
Voice: confusion of two
Who walk the daylight roads
Alone, wresting alone,

Yet meeting and parting, parting-
Meeting, till neither can see
In a stone stone, in a flame
Flame, but their tried selves

Lost in a stone flaming.

Terah

Before it can see the many
The mind blurs them to one
The better to cope with a separate enemy,
      friend, or truth —

                And when Terah returned,
All his idols lay slain except the high one
Standing erect, at its side
The murderer axe:
"Who have destroyed my gods?

"Abram my son, my son,
Have you killed your fears?

"Now you have cut them down, learn their faces!"

While the boy covered his eyes,
Terah lifting the slain presences could see
How the spilt breath was pulsating on their faces:
"Let them die there, son,
If their living stings your brain,
But you will father generations of terror.
Can one man's thought contain the world's?"

"He is one at last" the boy screamed.
The listening father pitied:
"If the many are one, your one is also the many"
And he shook with the breadth of the world.

Isaac

The story haunts this tribe that cannot wipe from its
      eyes
The flashing hill, the trembling man tying his son in
      his arms, the bewildered ram
Bearing twigs and firewood.   They think it again
      and again
Through fifty centuries.   Even now when they look at
      a chance hillock
Under the sky of an unmysterious day, the eyes
Of their poets hang it with flame —
                   "Father, father, save Isaac!"
One of them hears his night cry out, as though the
      indifferent cloud
Were sown with seeds of blood bursting to flutter
Over the boiling stones.

              Even my own father
One morning of my longago childhood helplessly
Watched his thought slip through the triple Hegelian
      chain
With which he wrestled the world, to relieve the curse
Thou shalt not raise thy hand . . .

                 Nor yet can a generation
Die without shouting once into the air to purge its heart
Of the blind obsessive tale, as though for always unsure
Of the wrong of worshipping the blood's terror of
      sacrifice.

What Plato Was

What Plato was I cannot know
Or care.   What Plato has become
Cleaves to me, bounds my days.   The form
Though bodiless as a glass of thoughts
Tortures the simple light that gushes
Out of omniscient suns to seek
My eyes.

          So will I strive to force
A second death against the looming
Bones out of whose partial glimmers
Chains of sons have recomposed
A crystal monster-lens.

               So must I
Work to bind into a final
Tomb all cleaving prism-forms
Through which the primal messages
Of day have been, will ever be,
Contorted, shriveled, seared into
A darkness-hallowed time-enthralling
Mind-reprieving balm.

Song of Succession

What am I doing, fiftyish,
Trespassing on your asphalt?   A shrewder animal
Would have found him a shroud and a hole long ago.

      Spare me
Your soft solemnities!   I have also believed
All you ought to believe now.   Hence, unless
         you're mouthing it,
Chase me out of your jungle!

         If I stand pat,
Crush my brain!   No loss to your possible world (years
Have cut too many tracks in its flesh: how could anyone
Heal caution's sickness now?)

            Then come, Oh drive me away,
Cleanse your street of me quickly!

       (But, careful: the plague —
       Better not come too close.)

              Make room, both of us,
For the unforeseeable few, for the headless guileless
      bodywise tainted multitude!

          Ready?

En l'an . . .

Autumn: paleness for men, harvest
    For planted field, for women
        Hollow calm,

When the curves of a narrowing sun fail
    To burn creation in two
        As in timeless summer:

Think? strive? Look back if only
    To gaze after something abandoned
        Vibrating still:

What if a ray's returning knowledge
    Grew in its eyes, asking?
        How would you answer?

"Wait"? — wait till after the coming
    Rigid gloom bursts
        With the swelling arcs

Of the always springing of the ice-flower?
    Would you cry out, again
        Call back, despite

All you have learned shivering beneath
    The fierce unseeing fires
        Of an animal sky?

(*For Dudley Fitts*)

Dialogue of the Stone Other

Friends are falling about me.   Some of them
Cannot get up from the ground.   Others
Rage stammering answers —

> *Man*
> *Smoothing your hair, standing before*
> *Your glass, charged with the burnt light*
> *Of the morning:*

Friends friends are falling:
What came on in blasts, swift,
Single — can it become the season
Of steady blight?   I —

> *Keep your eyeballs*
> *Fixed on its never-wavering —*

Friends
Are falling.   Merely to keep erect
May be a kind of youth.   Then —

> *Deafen*
> *Your ears to your own puff of words and —*

Friends are falling, falling —

> *Will you not*
> *Stop to hear your stone other*
> *That keeps on asking again again*
> *What will you do with its life?*

44

Time

Invisible vulture who cuts the day
From the night hangs over toiling-play
Until the inviolate act divides.

Talons tumble out of the air
On those who know and do not know
Whether they run away or hide.

Yet though the sufferers take the blow
As fate's redemptive surge of care,
Such unseen gatherings from the sky

Are the brain's mirage of a savior-lie
To victims scarred enough to dread
The power that a Rimbaud sought and fled.

In the Coastal Cities

Their ancient ancestors gave up hope of ever regaining
The first eden,
Yet the later ones believed,
Walking their years magnetized by faint impalpable rays
Of the second, after dying.

Now their children's children's children
Nurtured in want and hope can neither want nor hope
For any time to come.   Helplessness
Foams in their eyes, tightens their hands.   You can hear them
On the streets in the poisoned towns.
Their daylight breaks in black,
Their spring and summer scalded by wintered fire.
Getting and giving love,
They know each other by signs,

While you, lost in your own confusions of want and hope,
        ask of them
That they willingly wane in the streets
And wait while the elders stop the sea from invading
The land.   What if the elders fail,
If the land goes under?
If the sea spurts from groundholes onto the sidewalks?

Will of Choice

If you thought to name your course,
If you had the will of choice,
Would you stay where vertical stone,
Level asphalt, a dome of gas
Wall you away from your source
Yet hold a delirious force
That can slake for a time the thirst
In your cells of heart and brain

Or find a place outside
With the naked land? and hope
The plagues we bear may subside
Before the fever can creep
Through the slowly dying air
Into the roots of grain
And the skins of the planet prepare
To burst . . .

Chanson Innocente

Cast your faith in the ever-nearing
Catastrophe your brothers and I
Pull, each instant we live, down
On the mother-once sea, the nurturing sky,
The hostage acres of soil we flay
And beg for our bread and warmth.   Then hail
Catastrophe! — what else to hail
Except your terrified creature-lust

To survive?   Its imminence might save,
Driving, as with the wrath from a once-
Believed-in heaven, across the water
And land our all-devouring hordes
Till none could range but a remnant shriven
Of strangelove mind and suicide hand.

The Rock

I have looked all day for The Rock
In this land where the grains are always seen.
I found no mark on the soil,
Sand and loam too old once more to be pressed
          prone or pierced
Apart.   Only across the faces of scattered
Women and men are there any scars,
Rips, burrs — and these are such as a glacial mountain
Signs, roaring across dry ground to the sea
Of a younger land in the melting kill of its breath.

Sinai Foothills

Condor Festival

Herded the second month of each year
In fiesta, Indian mountain villagers
Learned from their alien lords who danced
A ring while axes bit at a tree
Ribboned with fruits and gifts till it flashed
To the ground.   Think of the Spaniard's trusted
Rite four hundred years ago

For chasing out pagan gods, when here
They hide in baited covered pits
On table-lands beyond their houses:
Indian mountain villagers watching
For condors.   When one nears they seize at him,
Rope his legs, carry him back
To the ring, and wait.   They cannot enter

The ritual ground until the villagers
Reaching above their heads have pillaged
All the gifts that hang from an arching
Pole. — But now they come.   Each holds
A condor wing; they bind the clattering
Feet to the tip of the arch.   Hungering
Human eyes watch him flailing

The air in a thundering will to soar
As horsemen with painted faces lunge at him,
Circle beneath his scorching eyes,
And then with their fists beat at the dangling
Defenceless head.   One of the horsemen,
Pressing his teeth to the gaping beak,
Rips out the condor's tongue.   The watchers

Shriek for the body, pounce for talismans. . .

50

III

Three Friends

We Brought You Away As Before . . .

We brought you away as before to return again
     with you here
But this time they knew you would have to be
     given a sleep beyond awakening.

And now we are back again, your three friends,
     in the same
City rooms, and everywhere your absence is an
     eyeless presence,

As though it might have been better if we had
     taken you away
To the wooded acres where you raced and wandered
     all the days long,
And had hollowed a passage in a corner of that earth
     and brought you there to quiet,

Or if instead we had set you free above, on the
     grasses,
And waited, watched, till your body fulfilled its
     own motion
Toward death, alone on your fields of home after your
     eight summer years.

Our Cat T.

Friend Across the Ocean

I go to my quiet bed, put out the light, prepare to sleep
And my friend across the ocean lies in his sickbed waiting-

Dying with nothing more to reach for, being cut away
A part of his body also: what was not taken is gnawing

The sane, and he does not know, in the blood's protection:
      peering
Into the faces that hover over him, trusting-believing

Their glance yet seeing mostly himself gazing from the pillow
      and past
The casement into the blackness of the London winter night–sky,

And mumbling again, as in manhood decades ago, *Verweile doch,
Du bist so schön,* love doubled back on itself as then; even

As now in my own body were it tied on a sickbed under
A gateless sky and not held back by the widening ocean.

W.J.B., 1894–1968

54

Wildness

We were together when we were young, and whatever the later
Moments of meeting, none of the burdens that the ticking grains
Had sown in the web of our separate skins could sever us.

I had told him long ago of something I had watched once
By a ruined wall of an ancient Italian town: a man
And a woman clinging together through flooding lava.   And still

They cling, behind a glass wall making them one, reach out
        seizing
Each other's safety against the sudden hideous thunder
Of kindred breath blown upward out of their trusted earth

To burst and descend as strangler-cloud.   He died alone:
What could he cling to who was always huddling close to the
        shadow
Of walls that keep out wildness — the world's, yours, his own?

But to die is to cast off dread: Wherefore now in the shielding
Crypt a quieter face lies parching, though the grasses already
Have come, have begun to invade and to take it back into
        wildness.

M.S.K., 1908–1967

55

IV

The Hero of Silence

*Scenes from an Imagined Life
of Mallarmé*

*The only thing a self-respecting
man can do is to keep looking up at
the sky as he dies of hunger.*
— MALLARMÉ TO CAZALIS, 1865

Dedication:
An Eternity of Words

So to compose the universe —
Killing:spawning worlds with denial,
Dragging truth through scourging laws
To earn a life in my thought.

What if the innocent blood of body's
Desire rise up in words unaided?
Even flesh can be burned
To the whitenesses of a song,

That out of oblivion ash may float
— My Orphic Book of the Earth! —
An eternity of words where naming
Creates, refusal destroys.

II. Master and Pupils

Time to lock up my brain and drudge to school.

Dare I ever cry out: "I own a glass
That sucks in eyes to the depths?"

Might they hear
If I began: "I found a curious thing
By chance —
Perhaps it came in a kind of trance" —
Thus easing the word, that they might care
This once . . .?

"A mirror, simply.   Familiar — but how to use it?
        Hear!
You must more-than-glance,
You must more-than-turn
When you look: Press, burn,
Stare them out of substance, enemy-loves,
Till the sight changes to sound,
Sound to nothingness —
The indifference of the sky, a stone" —

But none of them will care to follow me, captives
Of their own dismay,
Waiting inside this fatal door
For my entering step to trumpet daily war — Yet
Might I plead with them:

                    "Close your book
And hear of this glass I own.
It sucks all pressing eyes, presses them back

Till gaze parrying gaze
Bursts into ice of flame, to abolish walls,
Dissolve flesh into Azure" —

But no.   I am here.
Inside.   Against them now.

Gravely they throb: flesh I must love.   Has it overheard
My thought?

"It was only a mirror to me, to you,
Innocent glass but yet the defender of truth."

How they spurn!

"Open your pages!   Safer to eye a book!"

One refuses, begins to burn
Till I must stare him down.

Who is this other who presses back?   What wakes
In his eyes' answer?
What has he drawing me there
Through the mass of face dissolving?   Is light the youth?
Can I gaze it out of substance, flesh that trembles?

III. Soliloquy from a Window:
Man and Flowers

If flesh, then all that moves.   If blood, then juices
Of ground: blood of a tree, a rock, a flower,
    Of all who rise in the mist

Ever floating about a thought's secret
Abyss.   Manas converge to the point of light
    Vision flees when the fires

Of seer and seen entwine.   — Look at me, flowers
Beneath this window: calyx of roses, gold,
    Purple, white! Your multiple

Eyes, make me your mirror!   I dive within you
Bouquet: we return one another, flower and eye
    Moving from each to each

In wakefulness, one to the other's silence:
Song.   Shall we lose our flesh to dissolver-light,
    Starers become the stare?

You are shedding your faces.   Where have you gone, my petals?
Go to return, vanish as you return,
    So, live in a thrust of mind!

IV. Dialogue Before Waking

Stare! — Stare?

When you will
You can stare it out of substance —
Not only petals.

Whatever waits
For any man answers him with a face
Uplifted, throbbing to speak and be known.

And will you know them then
For what they are as they greet you,
Or must you hide from the ecstasies
Of touch? turn dazed by the flesh
You overlove in your dark of fear?

Stare!

Since you must, at last, at whatever face moves
        toward you.

Stare while the blood drains,
Forsakes the skin.

Then stare with the ice of thought
Fired with a love that kills, and watch the skin
Curl, twist, burn like paper; the bone
To ash —

And within that face
And out of that face that offered a trembling word . . .?

A hovering fume.

V. Fume

The air that hovered enters coldly,
Sounds in my brain suddenly —
      Nothing I heard before.

This is the silence thought can hear
From voices spoken by planets
      Scorching through nothingness —

Voice of the flame of sky!   Imagined
Flower of flame!   Floating
      Ideas of sound!   — Listen:

They throb alone, islands borne
In azure lakes, but glowing
      Fused and pure.   O Poem

Of Flight, I will you into words
From the nothingness of sense
      Through silences of sound,

Such as upon her wedding day
Cecilia, saint and blinded,
      Sang in her heart to God

Her song unheard.   Yet will I sing
Entwining sky and flower
      A flame that shall be heard!

VI. Into the Blond Torrent

Whatever palpitates lives: therefore threatens.
Name them all? — If naming alone could subdue!
 One of my waiting children
 Shall call them. All the equations

Exist. With our eyes' hot destruction we lift
Covers, so all that trembles can rise to the pure
 Reaching touch of kindred
 Selves. We have only to watch

To know. There is nothing left to create. We must see!
Unravel! vanquish! — even my innocent thirst
 For the flooding naked caresses
 Of her golden hair. Cover

My eyes? — Seize! drown! till the blond torrent
Bear me on her trembling thighs to the warm
 River of calm: the sleeping
 Ecstasy of the ages

Lost, found in her golden foam. O quivering
Gulf of invisible song! She alone — from her body's
 Vessel, let me tear out
 The dream! Let the waking phantom

Blind me! body burn with her flight! I shall plunge her
— Destruction be my Beatrice! — into the death
 Of love. And out of the blackness,
 Out of our blood silenced,

I may rise, victim, guarding the ash of her flame.

VII. The Waking

When body answered, blood
Rebelled,
Heart screeched at the ribs.

And when I uttered, vision
Burst.

And when I awoke,
I saw creation gaze on itself through me:
Infinity contained.

The dream that ravaged has remade.   Nothing
    can harm.
I hold in me a piece of the nothingness
Of which our night is made.

Agonized earth
Has vanquished under a vacant sky.

                                        O Poem
Of Flight, abolish wings!

I have no pain.   My mind
The hermit of its own purity,
Cannot be touched by time, cannot be touched
Even by time reflected in ageless shadow:
Day.

        I do not seek to make.   I seek
The freedom gathered, kept, and to replenish.
The finite falls about me till I die.

Note

Stéphane Mallarmé was born in Paris 1842, taught school for three decades until liberated from its enslavement in his fifty-second year. The meanings of his poems (some of which appeared after his death, in 1898) continue to be disputed. As for the "meaning" of his quest: though our scenes are wholly imagined, the language echoes words and thoughts that recur through his writings—such as mirror, flight, azure, woman's hair, absence, nothingness—as he moves from the "raw and immediate" world of sense toward pure idea, quintessence, blankness, silence.
Other passages of possible relevance to the seven scenes:

I. Tout, au monde, existe pour aboutir à un livre... L'explication orphique de la Terre, qui est le seul devoir du poète...

II. J'ai encore besoin... de me regarder dans cette glace pour penser... c'est t'apprendre que je suis maintenant impersonnel, et non plus Stéphane que tu as connu — mais une aptitude qu'a l'Univers Spirituel à se voir et à se développer, à travers ce qui fut moi... [Lettre à Cazalis, 1867]... O miroir!/ Eau froide par l'ennui dans ton cadre gelée/Que de fois et pendant les heures, désolée/Des songes et cherchant mes souvenirs qui sont/Comme des feuilles sous ta glace au trou profond,/Je m' apparus en toi comme une ombre lointaine... [Hérodiade]... Que la vitre soit l'art, soit la mysticité [Les Fenêtres].

III. Je dis: une fleur, et hors de l'oubli où ma voix relègue aucun contour, en tant que quelque chose d'autre que les calices sus, musicalement se lève, idée même et sauve, l'absente de tous bouquets.

IV. In approximate English: "What use of transposing a fact of nature unless the pure concept emanates from it . . . Thought that has thought itself through and reached a pure idea."

V. ...J'ai besoin de la plus silencieuse solitude de l'âme, et d'un oubli inconnu, pour entendre chanter en moi certaines notes mystérieuses [To Aubanel]... Le chant jaillit de source innée, antérieure à un concept, si purement que refléter au dehors mille rythmes d'images... Toute âme est une mélodie qu'il faut renouer... The invisible air, or song, beneath the words leads our divining eye from word to music . . .

VI. Le blond torrent de mes cheveux immaculés... Mais ta chevelure est une rivière tiède,/Où noyer sans frissons l'âme qui nous obsède/Et trouver ce Néant que tu ne connais pas!... La chevelure vol d'une flamme... Au ciel antérieur où fleurit la Beauté...

VII. Mon art est un impasse... Ici-bas est maître... We measure our finiteness against infinity [To Mauclair].

See also Notes (pp. 205 *ff.*) for pp. 59–66.

V

Second-Hand Poems

Más allá del amor

Everything threatens us:
time, that divides into living fragments
what I was
        from what I shall be,
as a cane-knife does with a snake;
consciousness: the transparency pierced,
the gaze become blind from watching itself gaze at itself;
words: gloves of grayness, dust of thought on the
      grass, water, skin;
our names, which rise up between the You and the I,
walls of emptiness, walls that no trumpet cuts down.

Neither dream with its population of shattered images,
nor delirium with its prophetic foam,
nor love with its teeth and claws are enough for us.
Beyond ourselves,
on the border between being and becoming,
a life more than life itself calls to us.
Outside: the night breathes, spreads out,
filled with great hot leaves,
with struggling mirrors:
fruits, talons, eyes, foliage,
flashing shoulders,
bodies that press their way within other bodies.

Lie down here on the edge of all this froth,
of all this life that does not know itself, yet surrenders:

you too are part of this night.
Stretch your full length, whiteness breathing,
throbbing, — O star divided,
wineglass,
bread that tips the scales toward the side of dawn,
moment of living flesh between this time and another
            measureless time.

ANDRÉ SPIRE

Retour des Martinets

Oh, at last you've arrived:
Arc in the sky, sparks, rockets
Loaded with all the warmth
And the chill freshness of mornings:
I watch from behind my window where the blooms
Of this late spring are beginning to burst.

Faithful guests, you're here again with your
        spurts of crying,
Your arrows hissing their laughter at me,
Your interlacings, your somersaults,
Your upward flights, and your tumblings —
Quivering imps of the sky!

What magnets? what breezes?
What mayflies draw you here?
Is it myself your harsh eyes crave?
Am I a friend, a brother,
An echo, a strain recovered?

I? — I, weighed down,
Eyes dimming,
Voice roughening,
Feet wavering,
Forehead doubting . . .

Oh, let me hurl back toward the ground
All hopes of flight that had budded in me
And plunge my envies and anguish
In the scalding waves of your endless assaults.

[*Written in the poet's 96th year*]

73

RAFAEL ALBERTI

El ángel mentiroso

And, I was broken,
not with violence:
with honey and words.

In the uninhabited wilds
of sand and wind,
a prisoner, alone,

I, somebody's shadow —
and a hundred doors of the centuries
walled up my blood.

O splendor!   Come to me!

Who was broken,
not with violence,
with honey and words.

RAFAEL ALBERTI

Canción del angel sin suerte

You are the one that keeps moving,
water that carries me along,
that will cast me aside.

Search for me in the wave.

The one that departs and does not return:
wind that in darkness
dies and reflames.

Search for me in the snow.

The one that no one can understand:
ever-inconstant presence
that speaks with no one.

Search for me in the air.

ÉMILE VERHAEREN

La Bêche

Frost hardens the waters; wind pales the clouds.

There: in the east of the field, in the harsh soil,
The spade rises and trembles
Pitiful, bare.

— Make a cross on the yellow soil
With your long hand,
You who depart by the road —

The thatched cottage green with damp
And its pair of lime trees struck by the lightning
And its ashes on the hearth
And its plaster pedestal still on the wall
But its Virgin fallen to the ground.

— Make a cross toward the thatched cottages
With your long hand of peace and light —

Dead toads in the ruts without end,
Dead fish in the reeds,
And then a cry ever weaker and slower from a bird,
An endless cry of agony from over there.

— Make a cross on the road
With your pitying hand —

In the stable's empty skylight
The spider has spun the star of dust;
And the twisted beams of the farm on the stream
Spring through the pitiful thatch
Like arms with the hands cut off.

— Make a cross upon the future,
A final cross with your hand —

Bare trees and severed trunks — a double row
Along the roads bewildered in their rout;
The villages — not even bells to ring
The hiccoughing hopeless *Day of Wrath*
To the empty echo and its broken mouths.

— Make a cross to the four corners of the horizon.

For this is the end of the fields and the end of evenings;
Mourning turns its black suns in the depths of the skies
Like millstones;
And only maggots come to life
In the rotten sides of women who are dead.

In the east of the field, in the harsh soil,
There: over the scattered corpse of the old ploughlands,
The spade, plate of bright steel, rod of cold wood,
Holds dominion forever.

ANNA AKHMATOVA

from "The White Flock"

For us to lose our pureness of words and of heart
Is what it would be for a painter to lose his sight
    Or an actor his motion and voice
Or a beautiful woman the radiance of her eyes.

But do not try to save for your private self
What was given you by heaven.   We are condemned
    — And we know it well — to squander
All we own, to keep nothing for ourselves.

Then walk alone, and bring to the blind their cure
Only to know in your aching hour of doubt
    The jeering malice of the few
You taught and the chill indifference of the many.

MIGUEL DE UNAMUNO

Me destierro . . .

I exile myself into memory,
I go to live on remembrance;
Seek me, if I am lost to you,
In the barren-wild of history.
For human life is sickness
And in living sick, I die;
I go then, go to the barrens
Where death itself will forget me.
And I take you with me, my brothers,
To people my desert land.
When you believe me most dead
I shall quiver in your hands.
Here I leave you my soul — a book,
A man — a true world.   O reader,
When all of you stirs as you read me,
It is I who am stirring within you.

PAUL ÉLUARD

Bonne Justice

It's the warm human law —
They make wine out of grapes,
Fire out of coal,
Men out of kisses.

It's the hard human law
To keep oneself whole
Despite misery, wars,
Despite death's dangers.

It's the soft human law
To change water into light,
Dream into fact,
And foes into brothers —

A law old and new
Ever perfecting
Itself from the depths of the
        child's heart
Up to reason supreme.

from

CAGED IN AN ANIMAL'S MIND

(1963)

*All thought is clay
And withered song*
— CLAY, p. 116

Historical Song of Then and Now

Earth early and huge,
No eye dared hope to travel
The palette of its rage

Till, late, they learned to wind
Shackles into its veins,
Shrank it to fit a cage.

So trust contracts to fear.
The tribes give up their feuds.
All wars are now one war.

And will you indict this breed
That strained against a code
Where safe-and-fed was good?

Fled from the mothering wood,
It found in its hand the thought
To light up endless day,

Revel with sleepless eye,
Make of itself a god,
And the veins a level sun —

Now it stumbles, dwarf in the maze
That the thinking hand had spun.
Blind in its blaze of stone,

Whom can this breed indict
That its sun is a blast of darkness,
That light is always night?

Ravel and Bind

Whatever: it bears a glow
Above; a seed below,
Thinking might never know
In like-unlike confined:

Lest it erupt and flow,
What can we make with mind
But sorts according to kind
From the worlds of ravel and bind.

Ancient of Nights

The broken wisdoms of the ancient lore
Float on the breath of night.   There is no road
Anywhere smitten with dark that you can tread
Safe from the swarm of glances that ensnare,

The instant day decays.   Try to enclose
A body of their fire! — a fleck of air
Blows in your hollow hand.   No sooner seize
A beadstring of those rays! — the staying stare

Mocks at your desperation; while they press
Steadily on your arms, against your hands,
Press in a time-dissolving wave that binds
Comfort and terror into a lost caress,

So glances enter though the clay defies:
The temple of the body's skin has eyes.

Symbol Curse

Tree and river = leaf and water?   Perhaps.
But after an instant's staring: matter and mold,
Then matter-mold shrunk to their sublimate,
Tree and river being too vast to hold.

I crush their sensuous presence so as to save
The fatal essence whispering into thought:
Symbol to me. . .   And what am I now to them?
But what I am to myself? — an aye, a given,
Standing for nothing more: the mere beholder,
To nothing — creature, life, or death — beholden?

Then die from me, symbol, die! that I may fly back
To you, water-and-leaf, river-and-tree,
Cured of the killing thought. . . .   I have you whole,
O pure presence swelling my ears and eyes!

Caged in an Animal's Mind

Caged in an animal's mind;
No wish to be more or else
Than I am: a smile and a grief
Of breath that thinks with its blood,

Yet straining despite: unsure
In my stir of festering will
Testing each day the skin
Of this wall for a possible scar

Where the questioning goad of the gale
Forever trying my bones
Might suddenly gather and flail
And burst through the wall. — Would rage

Be enough to hold me erect,
Dazed in the unknown light,
And drive me on with no more
Than my strength of naked will

To range the inhuman storm,
Follow wherever it lead
And answer — whether I hear
A Voice or only the voices

Of my own self-answering scream
In a void of punishing calm?

The Valley Between

Man with brow in the air,
Man with the spine erect,
Forepaws hung at the sides,
Drop your head to the grass:

What can you hear down there?
Nothing, nothing, nothing!
Listen, listen, listen,

Man with head in the air:
Raise it higher and higher
To the plain of alarming birds:
What can you hear up there?

Nothing, nothing, nothing!
Listen, listen, listen,
And hear whatever they are,

The voices calling you, calling
From the grass, from the plain of birds,
And up from the valley between
Where you batter a path alone

With your new-won stifle and knees.
Head unsure of the emblems
Unlinked to below or above,

Hearing no sound but its own,
Reels on the friendless shoulder;
Eyeballs riving with fear
Leap left, leap right, for the course,

While the shanks below push forward,
Right leg, left leg, forward,
Forward, endlessly forward,

Onward, endlessly onward . . .
Keep spine erect from falling!
Face from questioning backward!
So ever ahead and onward,

Onward, helplessly onward,
Onward, helplessly onward —

Thoughts about a Garden

Open windows and crack the cloud:
Strike!   It is never and always time —
Always never — the poles of a nothing

Between but a nonsense song, a nonsense
Cry of waiting.   Every moment
You suck in breath your life hangs

On a thread of air.   So breathe, speak,
That the thread hold, lest it snap and drop you
Gasping through seas of space.   Is your trust

Young enough to believe that flight
But one more storm and one more wave
To cast you up?   The sailor of Egypt

Sank from his shipwrecked boat in a gale's
Black to the island, slept with his heart
His lone companion, and so in peace

Beneath the night of a tree, ever
Embracing shade.   But your heart wavers
In any darkness on any shore:

Only your thought is sure — and thought
Hangs on a thread of air.   Then rush
Into the garden: crack a breach

In the wall of cloud that hides the always
And never answering ground of bloom.
Its truth hangs on your thread of thought:

Enter burdened with all you believe!

Petitioner Dogs

Much of the night we sleep
And we doze much of the day
And when awake we watch,
Eat, murder, or play.

Pathetic?   Quite.   We're dogs.
How could we hope to thrive
Blocked from the human secret?
Lend it! — we too shall live

Like you who dreams and knows
And dreads.   It is not too late
To muzzle our brains with grief
And thus rectify fate.

How long must we stay content
To drag our animal breath
From sleep to waking to sleep
In a practice of life and death?

You will guide, O friend?   Then begin:
While we vainly sniff at the air,
Let us vainly paw at the ground
Till we slobber in your despair.

Father-Stones

When all your gods have been carted away and the
        father-stones
Lie cracked into shapeless meal

And the iron mother-faces
Fester in red under dissolving waters —

Now when your leveled pantheon
Cannot enjoin even a wind, where will you turn,

Where will you look for the yes, the no, the possible,
Probable gate of light?

— Hack your way through arbors of discontent.

Night of the Canyon Sun

Lying above the rim
Of this hollowed world: my sight
Held in the never-believing
Night of this dark, suddenly
Floods with love for the sun.

But you, black sun, why you
Alone of the guardian terrors?
Beneficent sun, cold warmer,
Whose flood transfused to leaf
Propels the broods on earth?

Shall mouth resist with praise —
Mouth of your tissue — striving,
Fed on yourself, green sun,
Maker-sustainer?   I carry
Within the horns of my skin

The same pure arcs that listen
On the infinite's beach of fire,
The same forever wisdoms
Churning, out of whose gasps
The living and dying spheres

Unroll.   Then hail, my unquenchable
Day! white sun and only
Turner of sea-bed, mountain,
And helplessly flowing waters,
Whose law's caprice compels

Breathings of ice to burst
My axe of stone and knowledge.
O mountain- and vision-breaker,
How long will the heart stay blind
To your bitterly building might?

The moon is a frozen thought
But yours is the symbol fused
With the tendrils of its sign
So vastly strewn that desire,
Scanning the lights of dark,

Passed you by in the search
Of fire.   Eye of your flaming
Graces not mine alone
But drives me outward onward
To gather a calm that men

May grow when their bodies learn
To meet the guardian terrors
With unexalting prayer.
Wherefore, against all shadows,
In the hard plain light I cry:

"Consume-sustain your sun
That feeds and consumes our flesh!
Gorge on the bones for worship
And flee your dark!   Oh smother
The god in the sun with his passion

Not to adore: to know!"
An echo beats through the dark

From the wailing rites of fear
To maim the words of light:
"Never to know but adore."

— Speech falls back from the air,
From the canyon, into my ears.
Who will be heard: the shadows?
My sun of the desert night?
Till words are made to utter

Reverberations of light,
No man will speak to a man
Of what can only be found
In loneliness as he moves
Unaware in search of his heart.

A Recurring Vision

Down, down, gone down,
Gone down and under the sea,
Past harbor, streets, and piers — the sun
Has drowned.

So up with the lights,
Up, up in the streets!   Let cars
Dazzle at curbs, spit light, make a flare
For whatever man or woman gropes
In the alleys home.

You must drive out black:
Remember, its fingers would reach for your throat
At the death of day.   Black is cold
In a city of night or a cave.

Then light the stones
In all the storeys!   Turn up the bells
Of fire, tier on piling tier,
Till the panes burst and ring in the comfort
Of light — which is heat.   Turn on sound —
Its rays are warmth.   Pour it on floors
Till they shake the walls. — Look!   You live
Though the sun drowns in the sea. — Scorn!
You can tally survival, measure your miles
Of wire, tons of your stone, steel,
The heights and depths of quantified heat
That keeps your throbbing through nights of ice —

But sometimes
In the late morning I see your same stones wearing
Wreaths.   All through the day I see black webs
Hang from the towers, they sway from ledges, they are caught
In the hair of the ginkgo trees.   I watch them float on roofs
And swirl down toward pavements.   They crowd walls, every-
     where
Watching with an unknown unknowable stare
That eats at eyes that stare back till those eyes
To save themselves fling up
From the level below to the level above, to the sky, to a
     colorless foam
Above.   Whatever they find there
Soothes and holds them motionless.
Is it blankness of day? blankness of night?
A fiercer double disdain?

The Axe of Eden

And finally
The pure question that throbs under every facet
Of trust and bitten peace,
To ask of how and when,
Giving up all the wherefore-whys, outdistanced
Beyond all confrontation.
So prepare to enter: You must be asked,
Facing the face in the glass.

                    — There is no one there,
You expect to say; thus having clouded over
That a shape cannot break through.   It is always an image,
Never yourself itself.   Likeness
Is only a mask of thought, no touching fingers
To taunt you to hopefulness, madness, emptiness, sleeplessness.
You are withered enough to learn and you lack the years to
        evade.
What could you fear
That you have not already sustained?   By now you have died
All the imagined human deaths.   Who could devise
Wiser horror? — Then take your height in the glass,
Silver the back.   Gaze — and joy
In our innocent birthday song
        Out of the mud
        And into a field
        Lighted with trees and stones

Earth of the paradise — fen
To Eden — garden of faultless joy,
Teeming berry and leaf and flower
And over, under, around, and across,
Birds and angels flying the air —
They yellow down from the morning sun,

Scattering home through sleeping stars
— While your God was breathing, breathing out of His tree
Beneath whose branch you slept,
His sacred fruit above your head
In the evening air: apples of God,
Glistening always over your vacant eyelids,
Cluster of suns
Ever beyond the reach of arms,
The reach of eyes, dazed
In haloes burning the clustered branch,
Clustering mystic suns
Beyond the reach of thought —

                Where
Had your footsteps led?   From the garden wall
Had you spied the ravine beyond?   Your body
Shivered sleeping against the ground
The night you heard the branch sway down
To thrust into your hollow mind
The knowing suns, so into your veins
The birth of dream: *to seize beyond*
The reach, though seizing kill and spirit
Wail from its dying blood — to seize
His burning rose, swallow the fruit
Of God, His flesh infuse your flesh,
His sight your sight —

            The sacred tree
Twists the cluster high in a sudden
Scald of wind.   A fleering bird
Shakes you up from the ground.   And must your eyes
Surround your body's fear, watching
Shadows out of whose coil
May leap your double of dream?

99

                              Light
Breaks on the garden, bearing into your glances
Comforting shapes of day — yet the drugging dream
Hangs on your eyes.   And shall they always peer
Dreading the sudden seizing wraith,
The possible other of dream?

                    He is everywhere.   Fly!
Save yourself!   What are eyes against arms?   Fly!
Hide in the cave by the wall, and think, think
A waking dream to save.   Seize!   Kill
If you must — all is alive in this land but the stones.
Take one! harder, fiercer.   Raise it and strike!   But stop —
Everything bleeds.

                    Now you are safe, you can walk
With this axe of stone in your hand, back toward the tree
Breathing to you as before.   Shall you forget
It led you to an axe through a coiling thought
Of sleep to waking? — Before you walk,
Look at your hands.
Where will you wash the stain?
Eden's well dries up at the touch of blood.   Cross the walls
To the cataract in the ravine.   But once outside
Can you come back?

                    Go to God with your stain!
Ask who made you shed the blood.   Open your voice, accuse
The clustering suns that grew in your mind the sickness
        of dream.
Dare you believe Him innocent, you who were cast
In His shape?   You were shaped of Him by His Will
        in a pyre

Of yearning, lonely of God! All you have done is obey
The impulse under the image. Why be afraid?
He gave you fear. Is He in truth the God-
That-Makes? Then go in the helpless knowledge the suns
Compelled beneath your skin.

                        The axe cries out
Against the blight of this Eden Perfected — land
Of the paradigm void — if nothing dies
Nothing can spring to birth. The restless axe
Cries out for making. The edge that kills creates.
Who will hold back the hand straining to shape
The multiple dances?

                        — You have crossed the wall
To the cataract in the ravine where blood dissolves
Back to the sea from which you climbed
Out of the mud
And into a field
Lighted with trees and stones —
Fen to Eden's ultimate height. If anything shout
Into your ears that He drives you out of His garden,
Cry the Responsible God who prepared your flight
In the pyre that made you His double —

                        Puny creator,
Walking now with your axe beyond the ravines,
Beyond the cataract now —
Who could have ever believed this opening world of
        endless fields?
They would never have been believed, even from the farthest
        ledge
Of the garden wall. And now, lost in their midst,
How can your teeming eye and ear
Accept such oceans of grass burning a naked sun,

Vastnesses of fields and rivers and trees, rising mountains,
Magnificence of birth so wide and huge and far
And high — world without walls! trilling with cries, calls,
      screams,
Miracle wild of shape and wing.   Leaping creation.
Infinitudes for the possible . . .

                Does the axe
Know?   One might think it reasons,
The edge bubbled with rays, breathless
With force and flight.   Watch!   It is thundering toward
      you,
Surging over your head — your guardian!   Wake up,
This is no second nightmare.   You are no longer the child
Who cried for help in a poem that was prayer to Eden.
Nobody listens to cries in this goldening chaos,
Except his own.

           Yet scream if it brings relief,
Though yours are the only ears that turn, yours and your
      generations',
Milling through chartless paths that shape
The soil, multiple treading millions
Rising and dying in change and to each a pulsing
Axe, the body's stone extension that rises
To fall, to change, yet never to grow
A willing tongue of its own.   Yours
Is the single voice and still it shouts from the reckless rise into
      knowledge
Forever against yourself and your stone
In wavering love and dread of both —

Though you have done no wrong.   There is no evil
Except of a word you have made in fear.   There is no fear
Except in the wound of wraiths borne

From your pure equation of man with axe.   And are you sure
That pure is true, reasoning out of your cage
Of filaments attuned to your narrow gamut
Of voices here where the silence of night
Pounds the incessant torrent and beat, the blooming buzzing
        confusion
Past the filaments' deafness?

                                    And if you burst the cage
Into the day's torrent, would you grow sure? —
Messages beating into your ears,
Morning through night, starlight through sunrise,
Howling: screaming: cries of murdered ants and dying birds
        and failing grasses: explosions
In shrieking trees: in the spilling bloods of the billion creatures
        falling, rising, seen and unknown, near you, over you,
        under you —
You walk the earth with an axe.   Now it advances
Whirling over your head.
Acknowledge the stone, ask in the cage
Our only question: *Where?*

Though we tear at each other's tongues, we are the kindred
Of fear's confusion, given the range of a jungle
Unchartable, though the apertures of its sight
Would make of a point a sphere . . . the earth is round
And flat . . . each twilight we fall to wither reborn . . .
— Find the way through your dust,
Delusion done: Enter your tremulous wholeness:
The world is one and the world is a trillion fragments
Of touch.   Grow them together, cleave them apart —
They bear no scar: It is you, their maker-and-breaker-
And-healer.   Then press, cry
Against the cage till its agonized walls
Burst, and ravel and bind

Erupt in a flow of reason and blood's dissolving sea
Sight that makes and tears with a healing kiss —
Or, mute on land with fear,
Languish under your axe!

The myths
Denying change advance their sanctities
To ring you in a return to a God outgrown
And the priests you watched by the bloodfires on the swamps.
Must you flee them again, though swamp and fire
Had disappeared, had become night-past
Voids of fear?   Yet flee!   For ever the rites
Of terror wake, exhuming a primal dream
To strangle time and your history.

Everything made
Is good and sacred.   The paradise dream
Of childhood never was.   You were old
The instant you crossed the wall out of Eden,
Forehead gouged by compelling will to follow the sudden self
Boiling your veins.   O ancient face gorged with pain,
Beloved newborn face, look outward now and across
Your worlds within the world!   Admit no sin
But grief, no prayer but desire . . .   So turn eyes
With your making passion, and bear toward the multiple hills
Sight: and they shall be there as you build them there,
Though you die before or the clash of suns enshroud.
Truth is the truth of wish: direction is all.

Seedling Air

I do not change.   I grow
The kernel that my hair,
My thought, my blood, enflames.
I sing my seedling air:

I shout this ancient air

Into the hail of days
That washes through my skin
To pound and drench my bones.
I keep my light within:

My light burns on within

Flooding my endless rooms
Of pure and feeling brain
Till streams of wisdom-warmth
Murmur within each vein:

They chant within each vein

Will to withstand unchanged
All grindings of that air
Though torrents press down hail
Harsher than they would bear;

For what has will to bear

But outward change that strives
To enter in, and breath
But inner bloom that wavers
Under the hail of death?

(For Edward Dahlberg)

Revenant

To My Daughter: Eighteenth Winter

Who is that bird now whispering in the snow
With feet steady and young?   The violent glance
Battered you where you stood and sheared the air
With pain.   Follow those wings!   And if they dance

Headily into the iron mazes, hope
That the branch's spoke will bend, and if they leap
Into the gullies of snow, the lightless dunes
Will fold them in the humbling breath of sleep

Safe, never to rise, until your heart,
Shed at last of the stone of fear, can run
To seize a flyer of grief from a childhood's night,
Hallow the wings, shadow the bitter sun.

A River

Blue, windless and deep, above my head,
Above the valley, the plain, the distant trees:
    Depthless arch of a morning

September sky wherever I turn as I gaze
Upward.   From these peering ledges of rock
    To which my straying feet

Have borne my thoughtless body, let me gather
A blue world overhead, a green below,
    To carry back if I find

The path to home.   How did I travel here
So surely from the road through stumbling fields?
    What are those bending trees

Twisted across the slope below? — green granite
Arching a hollow?   Where does that sudden river
    Come from?   Where can it go?

Watched from this ledge below: see how it winds,
Sunk deep beneath its valleys, an ancient
    River.   But look! it curves

East and beyond.   Now it widens into a vast
Meadow of gray water?   Is it water,
    That flood of vacant light,

Or a withered field?   But there: it has filled the plain.
It is water. — But if water, how can it stare
    Into the deeps of the sky

With emptied colorless eyes?   Or is it blind:
River too old to bear an outward light,
        To carry blue to blue?

These must be the acres I wandered across
A year ago from a road far from my house
        When I followed into the blaze

Of a setting sun an unknown hurrying man,
The loom of fleshless form that gave no shadow
        Back to the dappled ground.

These trees covet their stillness, yet I ask
Their presences to warn me against my hour
        Of flight, early or late,

Before my body can gaze with empty eyes
And love become too inward borne to answer
        Light of a sun with light.

                    (For Allen Tate)

Seven

— And I was seven and I had seen
Shells in the hazel boughs: within
The outer shell a hidden tan-
Gold godlet eye winking, awaiting
Scramble of fingers to lay it bare
For the crush-caress of tooth and tongue

— Now I was seven: already old
In the taker's pleasure, and it was noon
And May and the hazel boughs of a year
Before were calling me into their day

— Then what was school or home or time
Or frantic mother tied to a clock
That tolled me late and lost or drowned,
When I might learn at the living shells
Starting now in bindings of green
The life from sleeping dark to sun,
Of silent growth to the patient pain
Of waiting to be found, adored,
And crushed at last to a death in joy?

Modes of Belief

Ever since I grew cold
In heart, I always hear
Most men that I behold
Cry like a creature caught
In tones of dying will,
Such as their eyelids bear
With cuneiforms of fail —

Where are the young and wild
Teeming in hope of power?
Though striving lifts the bud,
None can achieve the flower.
Where can the bud disperse
Within?   Must every man
Entomb a withered child? —

What early hearts can store
Of sweetness still endures
Fever of flood or drought,
Till groping up from within,
A self-bereaving curse
Masses in reefs of thought,
Burns and bites the blood —

(For Lionel Trilling)

III

Thoughts of the War
and My Daughter

The year you came to the world
Blood had already enflamed
The breath of a hundred cities,
Wounds of a thousand streets
Already stopped up, embalmed

In ash.   This side of the sea
We were June and green.   We could tell
Sleep from waking, in silence
Pure.   The wind blew east
From our rock-shelf, over the swale

Of ocean, never thrown back
To save: brittle and vain
With hope.   The year you babbled
The first of your words, you could play
Hide and seek with the rain

And his shadow — while we were learning
Fear, but slowly, crossed
In a weltering love.   You could prance
On fern and water, a spangle
Of sunlight endlessly kissed

By our eyes.   What was your thought
When you first looked overhead
And saw in a summer's field
Of night the ever-amazed
Face in a fleeing cloud?

The same as theirs, the children
With the tongueless women and men,
As they watched from the German walls
Over their death-camp cities
An ever-abandoned moon?

December 7, 1960

I Think among Blank Walls

Strive with reason under the open sky?
Landscape will spin your brain, wring your eye,
All knowledge floating weightless:

I think among blank walls
Bandied by sights whose spending clash ignites
A willing rapture, till the tongue recalls.

Surface

Less to uncharm the sea
Than to learn from a working sky,

I look at surface, trying
To see beyond or within

The stretch and bursting of skin
Whence every newborn wave

Tossed into air can thrive
Over an open grave.

Clay

To a snow-world deaf,
To a leaf-world blind,
Where can you go
With your dangling mind

Save to the hells
Of joy?   Then come
In your pith of fear
And your skin of numb:

The soothing tongues
Of blazing grief
May hollow your mind
Of its unbelief

In light and sound
And striving wish.
But do not covet
Your remnant ash,

Revel, or brood
In fire too long:
All thought is clay
And withered song

Whose sweet will burn
To a salt of truth
When leaf is age
And snow is youth.

Voyage: A Journal Entry

Every move out of darkness
Is a voyage into the sun —

"August 10.   Sun voyage.   Smithfield, Maine:

It began with wounds of light baring the trees
Across a misted lake, then it grew a morning . . .
Noon — blue endless revels in golden bays,

Then it rode a hugeball track down sky, past walls
Of horizon air and beyond — and a blind earth trembled
Till starlight rained from emerging heaven-hills —

End of voyage."   End — though the mind complain

And the will argue the hope of a love refrain:
End of faith that a more than gleaming of sky
Hallows a soil.   End — though the heart's disdain

Grant no mana to any light but the flare
Of human shadow clasped in the kiss of their singing-
Thinking fire.   End of belief in the sun.

House in St. Petersburg

If my mother had never been the protected child
Of a dreamy scholar in a protected house,
     I would not be writing these lines —

If the sign hung in the window of that house
Had told a different lie from the lie it told,
     I would not be writing these lines —

If the bribed police who winked at the sign had lived —
If the old one had not choked in a swilling night,
     I would not be writing these lines —

If the young recruit had been briefed with the well-bribed
       word
By his well-bribed captain before he walked by the house,

Or if he had never tripped on a cobble of ice
And ripped his shirt as he sprawled on a gashing stone,
     I would not be writing these lines —

If he had not then remembered the house with the sign
Because of the word it had always said to the street,

Or if when he asked the service of needle and thread
Father or child could have brought him needle and thread,
     I would not be writing these lines —

If the suddenly tongueless man of a stricken house
Had dared to speak with his eyes and a bag of gold,

Or if the gold had said to the young recruit
What it always said when the hunted spoke to the law,
     I would not be writing these lines —

If the young recruit had not shouted guilt in the street
So that passersby turned round to assault the house,

If he had not screamed the name as he climbed the steps
To the barracks and flung his find in his captain's face,

Or if when the captain scanned the innocent's eyes
He had found a gleam that confessed it was not too late,
        I would not be writing these lines —

If the innocent had not shouted again and again
And again — if the captain could have closed up his ears,

Or if his major, cursing his luck and loss,
Had never signed the papers to pillage and seize,
        I would not be writing these lines —

If the child and father, clinging with dread in the snows
Of night, had failed before they reached the frontier,

Or if their boat, lost in a wild North Sea,
Had not been sighted and saved on a Scottish shore,
        I would not be writing these lines —

Or, when they voyaged again, if their battered ship
Had not groped through its trial to the promised port,

Or if when they saw the sun of a friending earth
They had not danced in the recklessness of its air,
        I would not be writing these lines —

If the father after the years of dancing and grief
Had sought his sleep on an alien hill of Home,
        I would not be writing these lines —

Or if my mother, walking in tears from his grave,
Had not returned, one April, to join his sleep,
    I would not be writing these lines —

And if she herself, before, in a long ago,
Had never told this tale to a young one's eyes,
    I would not be singing her song.

Guide's Speech on a Road near Delphi

Stop the bus!   Then you will see. —
There, down there at the fork!

      Where?

Where the three roads meet, cross, join,
He killed, he struck.   Laius sauntering downward
But Oedipus racing up from the sea and raging
To flee whatever it was the oracle screechers
Showed him out of the fumes.   How could he stop,
Pelted by fear?   Why should he tack from the road
To let the hot-tongued menacer pass?   Old men
Are full of time — but the young? . . . He flails, he slashes,
Bodies skid to the ground.   And he could not look,
His eyes on a string to Delphi, twenty-one miles
And uphill always.   He leaps with his horse —

      The myth
      Is true?

You ask! — One makes a choice.   Yours?
"A winter's song" perhaps?   You shake your head,
Believing nothing.   But I believe it all,
Watching this light each day.   There are no myths:
Everything happens.   Live long enough: you shall see!

Summer

Summer is here — gone is a carol's search —
And light is everywhere: his breadth and height
Dazes the world.   What if this vastness scorch
My lids of flesh?   Its hour will come for flight.

The hour is near — what would a carol bring?

A wind of birds crushes against the night,
Its seeing stones are falling —

                        Cling, O cling,
Voice of my dark, even with blinded sight!
What if this summer cinder to eyeless white
The lavas of color glorying on your wing:

My earth must die in black.

                        Till then, sing, sing,
Voices — my darkness striving to be light!

Midnight Wind to the Tossed

I glared at the wind, the wind glared back.   The window
Walls us apart.   Where have you gone? — No answer.
Better that way.   A truce is made, the issue
Thrown to a farther night.   At last: good-night!
But fire comes creeping into the sky, the room,
Eyelids.   Oh, what are walls?   "Scatter their stones!"
Why?   "For the reachless roses.   Wake up!"   Roses?
        "And listen:

A free man needs no house: only a fool
Lusts in rooms for calm: only the old
And young can always sleep: only, the tossed
Wrestle with shadows, striving to close fingers
On shapes of loving.   Wake!   To be purely free,
Speak to your hands until they drop from your arms.
Cherishing is to touch, covet, and seize."

Listen:

(On a spring day in 1853 Gérard de Nerval set out to visit Heinrich Heine, but he lost his way in the Paris streets, wandered, and stopped in despair. Finding himself near Notre-Dame de Lorette, he entered the church and began to confess. Then a voice within him said: "The Virgin is dead; your prayers are useless." Some hours later he loitered at the Place de la Concorde, his mind filling with thoughts of suicide. But each time that he started toward the river, something restrained him. Then he looked up at the sky and saw a vision: "Eternal night is beginning," he said to himself. He turned again through the streets and after long wandering, he found his own room and fell asleep. When he woke, he was startled to see the sun in the sky and to hear shouts of "Christe! Christe!" from children below his window. "They don't know it yet," he said to himself, "but Christ is no more." An hour later he was dressed and in the street and on his way to Heine's rooms.)

His knock at last, my Genius — and still I dread it
Fiercely with love.   What will he bring me today?
Another claw from the sea?   Rags?   Or a bird
Bearing its little death?   "Those are not eyeballs!
Planets!" Gérard will whisper.   How he will sob
Until I comfort his grief with "It's true!" — near God
Of the Gentiles, lend me your calm! — and grant him light
Yet not too much, this delicate poor Jesus
Of the burning storms, who sees with single eyes
Your double world.   Would I might also —

Nerval's speeches are enclosed in double quotation marks;
Matilde's in single; Heine's are set in italics.

124

Gérard,
Here so soon?   Come in!   But what are you clutching
So tenderly in your hand?

"I think I saw a black sun in the deserted sky.
The black sun changed to a bloody globe.
It was hanging above the Tuileries —"

Just now?

"Everything lives, everything stirs:
All is answering all.
That is not madness."

Madness, Gérard, madness?
If only I might look with your eyes, and find!

"See, with your own!"

I peer, but the fire is cold.

"Why, then, are you smiling?"

Is this a smile:
A Jew's deathly grimace against himself?

"Man is double.   Never contract to a one!
I know.   I have watched me flying away while I stayed.
You have read my report."

Of course.

"Then, touch the string —
This that I hold in my hand."

How, when you clutch it?

"The string: my treasure. But first, look with your eyes,
With all your sight! Strain! Force! and again! —
Good. And now you can know."

But what?

"Now take it,
Touch it. Then give it back. At last in my hand:
The string from her girdle: Cleopatra's: hers
And now my own. Her girdle about my throat,
I wind it — thus! Listen:"

Stop! Let me hold it!

"Gentle."

Come, I shall save it here for you.

"No.
I need it. I found it at last. The search was long."

No! Wait — someone is knocking outside!

"The search, the search —
And now no more to search — "

The door, Gérard.   I must answer.

"Someone and no one, always.
Send him away!   Listen, I bring the Secret."

*Of course — in a moment.   I shall be back.   Stay there!
There, that chair!   An instant — no more!*

(No more —
An instant!   Now think, oh think, and act!   The string!
Seize it now?   It is — no, I can see it.   My God,
I see him: he has found out his Sacred Thread —
He will twist it around his throat —)

Mathilda, Matilde!

(If I reason — but could he hear me?   And now?   What
      now?)

'You shouted.   Why?'

*Shouted, Matilde?   Shouted?
I am thinking — in a mistake ...*

'Is he well today?'

Superb!

'Then I'll go back.'

*Yes, no, wait — wait!
I may need you.   Wait.   Let me think.   Kind God, must
      he die?*

127

'Is he lost?'

Gérard?   Am I lost?   Shall we ever be found?

'Listen!'

To you?   No.   Go to the street — a cab
For the hospital!   Dubois! a cab!   Matilde,
Hurry!

'At once.'

Hospital, hurry — save him!

'Go to him, then, and wait.   I'll call you.'

Gérard,
Nobody knocked.   I sent him away.   Now, tell me again.
*   I am here.*

"The Secret?
   Listen — but be calm!   It is all explained.
   Listen, and gently listen:"

(Oh what have I done?
What am I doing?   Take me away instead!
I am the madman.   I, of the Tribe of Dream,
Summon my Enemy-Sane to lock up the Dreamer. —
O traitor-and-coward God
Of my fathers, forgive this crime, for you are the guilty
Condemner of all my fathers and fathers and fathers
In the ancient jails of our fear where the only tools

For keeping alive were the scissors of ghetto-wit
Honed on our skins of pain.   Praise yourself, God:
One of your chosen at last comes through to defy —
One of the terrified nurslings
Carrying yet in his blood the stifler-and-poison
Caution, and only faith in the things they can touch,
Taste, smell, use, and break with the tester's eye.
And what of the plundering truth
In vision the reckless behold?   Am I exiled forever,
Never to find what they find in a boiling brain?
Never to dare the passion? — A poet, I?
Spilling tunes on the toes of the claybound tribe,
Seer of the semi-blind? — Must I forgive,
Jahweh, the Safety-God? —)

'Henri, wake up!   They are here!'

Too soon.

"Who?"

Gérard, we must take you.

"Where?
I am here."

You are lost.

"Lost?   No, I am saved.
You have believed my eyes."

Come with me, friend!

"Must I come?"

Give me the string.

"It is here — it is mine!"

It is yours and I will protect it.   All shall be safe.

"But no.   Wait — I must tell you the Secret.   Listen:"

Time Is a Double Line

*(From the unwritten account of Don Isaac Abravanel:
diplomat, financier, mystic)*

I INQUISITION EVE

Talked with the King today — and he lied, as always
"Then I begged the Queen," I said, "She tells me *The Lord
Has put this thing in your heart.*   So today I beg
Nothing.   I come to purchase, purchase from the King
A word: that the people stay."

                    "And we merely marvel
How you of all men could so misappraise their worth!"

"They can bring no more.   Nor need you suspect they hide,
Bribe, withhold.   I give you my honor —
Here; it lies at your feet."

"I should rather take something else: Faith.
Trust me with yours, as the others have done!
Place it here in this hand, that your King
Might be your sponsor.   Speak!"

                    "I speak what the Queen
Spoke of your own heart: hear — *It is in the hands
Of the Lord, as the rivers of water.   The Lord turns it
Whithersoever He will,* so He turns the hearts

Of those I come to ransom.   Give your command
And each of these men will bring you sacks of gold
Grateful to serve in pride."

                "You offer me bodies —
Why?   I am looking for souls.   Come back tomorrow,
And let the Lord make yours ready!"

II SPEECH BEFORE EXILE

           — Time to fly
Out of this loving land into a loving dark,
Fly in joy though my people scream at the sea.
"Where?" they will moan.   I must show them:

           — What can it matter?
We have only a handful of years to wait till this earth
Leaps into fiery blossoms.   Lucky for us
A king of dust cannot read the dial of the heavens:
Messiah is moving so near we can count his moons —
Eleven holy years
Of exile and then the first of the hours of bliss:

           Oh, look to their East!
Rome is on fire, the dust is a hail of brimstone,
Tiber is burning pitch!   The Avenger has come.
Can you see it now? — Then store a coal of that sun
Into your hearts and keep it blown as we sink
Into the blackest sea of our grief.   We shall wade its wave
And land be dry to our feet.   We shall strive in joy,
Burning blood in this last of the trials of blood —
The last, fiercest to bear.

132

But time is a line,
I have measured its end: darkness dies at the burst
Of the light.   What if your throats gag with your hate?
Our veins are filling up with night.   Beware:
That night can blacken your brain unless it is blazed
With the coal of love.   Then sing in our blood as we rage,
And think in our veins till the light without and within
Suddenly opens earth to our joy, man to his day.   Then sing,
Shout, as we march: *Time, time is a line,*
We have measured its end, its end — Time is a line:
Blackness dies at the burst of the light, the light.
Shout, people, sing! —

III   BEYOND THE GRAVE

How have I wandered into the voice
Of those who strangle the dead, craving
To hear their own thought's echo echoed?
And must I hear the words they hear me say

While here I wait, rethinking my days, five centuries
Beyond, and dead?

                O time,
The living say we make them your slave with our histories,
Yet how else learn beginning, middle, and end —
How else imagine?

                More than cold eyes can know,
There are two of you in your one: time of the brain
Notching days for account,
But the other, not an arithmetic, in the blood:
So blood is soul and blood is endless: my own

Mixed in the fume of all, to a stone, a tree,
To the river of my vein.

        Yet could I have lived
Five centuries beyond that flicker of days,
Or five or ten before, if I had known you,
Time of the timeless blood?   Wherefore I ask,
Now in the warm blood-knowledge of ever-entering eyes,
How to speak what I see:

(For Ben-Zion Netanyahu)

ANNA AKHMATOVA

The Muse

When in the night I await her coming,
My life seems stopped.   I ask myself: What
Are tributes, freedom, or youth compared
To this treasured friend holding a flute?
Look, she's coming!   She throws off her veil
And watches me, steady and long.   I say:
"Was it you who dictated to Dante the pages
Of Hell?"   And she answers: "I am the one."

Denk nicht zu viel ...

Do not ponder too much
Meanings that cannot be found —
The symbol-scenes that no man understands:

The wild swan that you shot, that you kept alive
In the yard, for a while, with shattered wing —
He reminded you, you said, of a faraway creature:
Your kindred self that you had destroyed in him.
He languished with neither thanks for your care nor rancor,
But when his dying came,
His fading eye rebuked you for driving him now
Out of a known into a new cycle of things.

PAUL ÉLUARD

L'Amoureuse

She stands upon my eyelids
And her hair is in my hair,
Her shape the shape of my hands,
Her hue the hue of my eyes,
She is swallowed up in my shadow
Like a stone upon the sky.

Her eyes are always open
And she does not let me sleep.
Her dreams in full daylight
Make suns burn up in mist,
And make me laugh, weep and laugh,
And talk with nothing to say.

PAUL ÉLUARD

Passer

Thunder hid behind black hands

Thunder hanged itself at the main gateway
Madmen's fire is no longer haunted the fire is wretched

Storm slipped into the tombs of the cities
Fringed itself with smoke crowned itself with ashes
The paralyzed wind crushes faces now

Light has congealed the prettiest houses

Light has splintered the woods the seas the stones
The linen of golden loves is now in shreds

Rain overturned the light and the flowers
Birds fish are mingling in the filth

Rain has run through all the highways of the blood
Washed away the pattern that guided the living.

HUGO VON HOFMANNSTHAL

Eigene Sprache

As words grew in your mouth,
Now a chain has grown in your hand;
Pull the universe toward you!
Pull or be dragged!

ANDRÉ SPIRE

Quand midi t'allonge à terre...

When noon hurls your body against the ground,
Sweating,
Your ears humming,
In the midst of bees that trample down
Swollen aloes and lavender,
In the midst of ants, resins,
Pine cones, thickening saps, outspread petals,
And below your feet, the ocean
Sleeping in stupor among the reddened rocks —

When noon glues your body against the ground,
In the midst of hunched and muted birds,
Your shirt burning your skin, your throat dry,
Your mouth parching, your neck numbed, your eyes
Blinded, your brain drained,

Know and behold your god!

RAFAEL ALBERTI

El ángel bueno

One year, when I lay sleeping,
someone — an unexpected
someone — stopped at my window.

"Rise up!"   And lo! my eyes
were beholding feathers and swords.

Behind: mountains and oceans,
clouds, peaks, and wings,
the sunsets, the dawns.

"Gaze on her there!   Her dream
is dangling from nothingness."

"Oh yearning, steadfast marble,
steadfast light, and steadfast
movable tides of my spirit!"

Somebody cried: "Rise up!"
And I found myself in your presence.

from

EARLY AND LATE
TESTAMENT

(1952)

The poetries of speech
Are acts of thinking love
— POETRY: THE ART, p. 147

Poetry: The Art

In the Form of an Apostrophe to Whitman

I used to read your book and hear your words
Explode in me and blast new passageways
Deep in my brain, until its crowding rooms
Held more light than my head could balance.   Now
That the tunnels all are cut, I pace the rooms
Looking for you, though certain I shall find
No more of you than you yourself could gather
Out of the pieces of self.   The years have burned
The sharpness from the edges: I can fit
The pieces, but the mortar must be mixed
Out of our blending wills.   Others have tried
And failed.   I too shall fail if I forget
How thought can range beyond the last frontiers
That common sense has civilized with names.

Others who looked for you have made you say
Words you might have said if they were you:
Have lost you in their passion for a phrase.
The private man's infinitude defies
The singleness they look for when they strive
To sort your various colors to a scheme
Of thought-and-action.   Desperate for pattern,
They make the key *Calamus* and they twist
Your other selves around the centerpiece,
Losing you in that love.

                    And others forge
A key of social thought that cracks apart

When words and actions contradict: *Walt Whitman,*
You said you love the common man!   Where were you
When Parsons' friends were hanged?   Were you asleep
Or writing more fine words about mechanics
And farmers? — How much cosier for you
To prate about democracy than live it —
You, its self-appointed poet!

                    Others,
Seeking you in your plangent celebrations
Of science and the holiness of flesh
And earth, end with a fierce *You too, Walt Whitman,*
You flinched, you stumbled, hankering for a "soul" . . .
The substances of sense too harsh too bitter
A truth for you to live by!   Underneath
Your protest boils the soft romantic sickness
Of all the Shelleys, Heines — bright lost leaders
We hoped were men.   You were afraid of the dark:
You who had thundered "Science is true religion"
Sang the groveler's wooing song to Death
And God and Spirit! . . .   Hide, at least, the image
Revealed: the gaudy chaos of a man
Reviling his own faith!

                    But who can dare
To arbitrate the depths of you that anger
Against your tranquil self?   I am not certain:
I have seen the signposts of contradiction
Planted by men impotent to discern
The harmony beneath the subtle wholeness,
And in their self-defence erect confusion

On quiet entities.   A poet's words
Are signatures of self — the many selves
Subsumed in one profounder sense that knows
An all-according truth: a single eye
Uncovering the countless constellations
Of heart and mind.   Wherefore the syllables
Reach outward from the self in an embrace
Of multitudes.   The poetries of speech
Are acts of thinking love; and I must find
The thought that grows the center of your passion.

And so I say to those who precontemn
The message of *Calamus* as the flowers
Of twisted love what Plato showed of truths
Uttered by poets.   And I say to those
Who spit upon your social thought *"Respondez!"*
The human race is restive, on the watch
For some new era — some divine war —
Whose triumph will entrench a brave good-will
Among the common people everywhere —
The trodden multitudes for whom you clamored
A new and tender reverence.

But for those
Who sneer because you looked for lights beyond
The planes of sense, there is no final answer
If they deny the mind its birthright freedom
To range all worlds of thought and sense and vision.
Everything that can be believ'd is an image of truth —
The images refined to great and small

Will cluster into orbits of belief
And hold together as the planets hold
By kinship and denial, in one vaster
All encompassing circle.   Let the sneerers
Proclaim your chief intent or keep their silence
Until its name is found.

                    It is not found,
The answer to your central search — "the problem,
The only one" — *adjust the individual*
Into the mass.   For we have just begun
To fit the world to men, men to the world;
And we shall stumble till the single heart
Discovers all its selves and learns therefrom
How singleness and multitude can live
In valiant marriage.   With your hungry hope
You pierced the shells of feeling, trumpeted
Into your country's ears, and flooded strength
Into the wavering hearts of men lonely
For courage to fulfill their need: to thrust
Their single faith against the massed-up wills
Of many.   "Sing your self!" you told them.   Listening,
They pledged the valors of the inward man.
And others turned from you with dull, deaf ears,
Afraid to listen, waiting to be taught
The trial-and-error way of rats in a maze . . .

A poem "is," some men believe.   I say
A poem "is" when it has spread its root
Inside a listener's thought and grows a tree there
Strong enough to burst a room in the brain,

And bring its branch to blossom.   Then the host
Forgets the verse and ponders on the mind
That made this seed of growth . . . as I forget
Your poem: as I strive to learn your mind,
Thinking that when I come to understand,
I may begin to touch serenities
You saw beneath the springs of pain that nourished
Your world that was beginning — dim, green world
Trembling with death-and-birth: divinest war.

Time of Brightness

Before it happens, before the sudden destruction
By your own hands or another's, let it be told.
It is better to know than to mourn what never was.
There is too much brightness here.   Look at the leaves.
Green light burns your eyeballs; the lids close down
To open darkness.   There at least you can see.

Figures are swimming up from nothingness.   Reach for them!
What if they twist and slither away the instant
You strive for a catch, like the withering purple shapes
Staring up under sea waves: something is there
To be sought and known.   You knew the dark before
The explosion into light; you read the outlines
Once.   Are those eyes now lost?

It was not always
This bright on earth.   You could image shape, you could tell
A cloud from a stone when you cared to look.   What was it
Prodded your sleep into waking, shaped on your tongue
Words to be said to earth, your discovered home,
Syllables of serenity such as a man
Sure in belief could say to a more-than-loved

> *For you must always be a moving song*
> *And we must always follow for your sound*

Nothing under the words? — It is not too late
To strain for remembered sight . . . or are the eyes
Grown alien to lost colors past estrangement?

There still is darkness in your veins, alive
With early voices: Hear, if you cannot see!

> *There was a wail of quiet.   Then I heard*
> *A rat's white, hollow strumming on the floor.*
> *The tent-flaps rumbled in a husky word*
> *Born of a wind's last roar —*
> *While up above the shore*
> *Wet webby grayness skidded down a tree*
> *And wrapped the water's limbs in curdling cold.*
> *Then like a cry crackling the slow sea*
> *A sling of sunflame whipped the gray to gold —*

Children voices we have used for gracing
The walls of our hollow houses, slender songs
Drifting across the waters of darkness, covering
The heavier sounds of a later, desperate wish:
Save them for a season of calm, for a time
You can dare to revel again when a rush of leaves
Falls in a shower of music to the ground.
Turn from them now: listen for what lies under them:
There is still time, the sounds may still be alive,
You may hear them yet or think you hear — but if only
The sudden beat of blankness floods your ear, come back,
Come out of the dark and into the loud light.
Reason-mind is not wholly weak; it can tell
High from low and the gross distinct; it must tell:
There is nothing else to know with, now that the reach
Of eye and ear is cut.

You will move slowly
This mind has no muscle of flight; it plods the ground

Traversed before.　Trust it to trace the imprint
Of the signatures before and reconstruct
Your early and later testaments.　It is safer
To crawl and think with this earthbound light, searching
Through tedious streets than to dream at an ocean's edge
For a possible heavenly answer traced in air
By a wind that drags a cold wave's moonwhite hair.

Hero Statues

Though bosomed by the same ground
And driven by the same sun,
A wolf no more assigns
His safety to a man,

Than man, whose lifted hope,
Dazzled by heaven and hell,
Can trust his fate to heroes
To do with as they will.

Now in an hour of frenzy
To find a vaster worth
Than death-through-fear the fathers
Decreed for man on earth

They smash the hero statues,
Accuse the idiot lust,
Spit in the tombs of glory
That canonize distrust,

Summon the world to cancel
Truce with murderer-dust.

Dialogue of the Heartbeat

I

The sun came up at five o'clock,
At six o'clock the sun went down;
None of us saw it, no one alive
Here or in any town.
Clenched in the stone of our will, we forgot to look,
We forgot to remember.   We always forget to remember.

It is warm and safe in our private room.   We can hear
Syllables of our mouths; we watch and reach for
Words of our lips: invisible flowers floating
In our glitter air, shaking us with their spells.
Is it not good, this air in the stone house
Of our will?   It is richer than any outer air,
Than perfume of raindrenched grass on October mornings,
The steady helpless breathing of wind against trees:
It is brighter than any brightness of outer air.

II

Clouds on a winter night
Can blot out all the stars
And cover up the moon,
Backed by the bitter force
Of wildly gathering air:

So, when invisible wind
Drives to the level crust
Of ground, no living bastion
Hopes to hold back the thrust

But shudders under the weight
Of plunging tons of sky
That shake the iron hills
Like soft black miles of sea,

That stun rock-rooted trees
Powerless under the might,
And draw from their birdless boughs
Weak cries against the night

Such as a man might utter
In helplessness to defy
With the summoned battalions of thought
The brute will of the sky.

The Bridge

We build a bridgehead from here and now to tomorrow.
Can you hear the word its gesture speaks
As it towers over us, tall, huge,
Cutting the sky with its head,
Pressing the ground with its feet?   Is it running
Across the water, charging
To span the sea in a leap?

Does it say we must seize tomorrow,
Tear it out of the air, compel the future
To come to us here and now?
Does it say we must stand and make eyes ready
To know the new as swift light swims
Slowly up from the darkness: wait, hope, listen?

Or would it say: Hungering hands
Can tear at mists, but passion is not enough:
Tomorrow eludes the blind wild will, yet silence
Waiting passive in hope can never grow
Creation out of the air?   Has it said to you: Quicken
Your blood with enormous thought: tomorrow listens?

Our bridgehead leans toward the far horizon
To mix with a far light flooding.   Look, the arms
Reach out to greet the future: outstretched arms
On whose young strength we hang our road
Till tomorrow raise a bridgehead:
Tomorrow also stand with outstretched arms
That the two bridgeheads may meet, the old and the new
Join hands to close the ocean.

You see no light, you say?
Nothing beyond?   No bridge?

No outstretched arms? — We see it
Whether or not they range the air: half of whatever we see
Glows in cells not signalled by our eyes.
If men lived only by the things they knew
The skin of their hands could touch, they soon would die
Of starved need.   The shapes of sensate truth
Bristle with harshness.   Eyeballs would cut on the edges
Of naked fact and bleed.   The thoughtful vision
Projected by our driving hope creates
A world where truth is possible: without it
The mind would break or die.

Looking for Papa

I

The clear white waters of the moon
Double in hills the earth-shadow more
Than the metallic flaming sun
Or the most frozen star.

You who seek an altar-god,
Turn from the stars, turn from the sun;
Though suckled by the mother sun,
Fly to the moon:

There you can learn the mystery
Whereof the best of gods are made —
Beautiful coldness, and over all
A strange shade.

All the sad young men are looking for papa,
The sad young men who think they were bad young men,
And their fathers and their grandfathers who were young
Once and are old: all the old young men,
And the women too, and the children: every one —
They are all looking for papa ... burdened papa,
Helplessly procreant papa who never was born
Or found.
   Shall we join the hunt? Is it a game?
A wonderfully solemn game, and very sad.

Let's look for him then. In the sky, in the sea, in the ground,
Any where at all, above us, below us, so long
As we look outside. Be sure to look outside
Ourselves. . . . Poor wandering papa,
Bright and invincible and always outside, always outside;
We must never allow him entry; we must never
   let him come in.

Among Trees of Light

Always men on earth have sought the wondrous
Mist-shadows for sacredness; all else lay
Too far from heaven:

In the night's darkness, we said, are symbols stranger
Than ever day with all its magic and dazzle
Could hide away.

Older now with empty hands, emerged from darkness,
We move among trees of light, striving to learn
The flaming mind

That beats in every glitter of day; we gather
Figures of light none of the dark's adept
Could find, fond

In the shadow-mists.   Searching till leaves lay bare
Their sleeping suns, we dare accept as much
As fire unlocked

Can show, however the embers freeze or scorch us,
Fearful that eyes alone, or thought, or love
Alone, can capture

Nothing beyond the reaches of singleness:
Not light but the mirrored glow of a burning wish.

The Fear

A Sonnet to the Earth

Because your flame was torn from burning skies
And spun in space to find the course or fail,
We cannot look at you with children's eyes —
For we are children of the same travail;
Nor can we let our calm become too strong
Or build contentments in the path we found,
For you must always be a moving song
And we must always follow for your sound.

Though yielded to your song's enchantment, none
In our tribe of flesh can give his heart's release
To certainties — thus do we mock or wrong
Your will, torn by our fear of stark caprice
That questions why we follow in your song
Arcs that may break us both against the sun.

Coasts of Darkness

A tribe of hearts will endure
A chartless night unknown.
Drawn toward the coasts of darkness,
No man who starts alone
Bondless returns unbroken,
Though first his heart rejoice,
Freed from human speeches
That had always muffled the silence —
Now he will know its voice

Rousing his sleeping wraths,
Ringing gongs of his hate:
They close in around and above him
Blindingly while they wait
For the torment in his blood
To strangle his bondless heart
Till it plead to mercies that scorn him —
Then can his frenzies start:

Moon, from your dizzy ledge,
O scream through his crazy night!
Spill through weird shaking trees
Live stones of bleeding light!
Swift through his eyeballs level
Beams that may pierce his skull:
Nail down his feet, moon, possess him
Till he is glutted full.

And then if his blood still fevers
To brave alone the wild ground,
Flood through his mouth till his body,
Freezing and burst by your flaming,
Screams for your love and is drowned.

I Build My House . . .

I build my house to keep out vermin, damp,
Decay, and time.   Poems embalm belief
With words; paintings lay out the growing brightness
In shrouds of color; sculptures mummify
Flesh softness into rock.   Can a daisy think?
Whatever is learned at last, we alone can summon
Fire, can touch a match to the logs and quicken
A cold black house with locked-up light of the sun.

Once in a dream I searched a globe, holding
Candles to see whatever might wait within.
Trustful, I pried at the sphere, tore it,
Looked inside.   It was empty dark:
Hollow earth of nothingness in the core.

Waking, I walked to the window; looked at the sky
Of morning overhead and the growing brightness
Below.   My land was alive:
Miracle breathings of flesh and leaf joining
Voices in dearness everywhere.

There is no wasted land until we cover it
With dryness of the heart in weariness,
Deny our anchorage to a land bedded
On a basalt continent that turns on seas
Distilled from waters blown from a time and place
We can never reach or touch, propelled by light
Of a sun beyond beholding: circled flesh
Contained within a sphere, straining to tear

Through the shell, range the beyond, and flee the hollow
Nothingness of the core.

Open your eyes
To the words, the rock, the color; take what they hold
Of fever-summoned calmness — more than enough
To quicken and sustain the truce you need.
Accept them: they are all you have, though flawed
By desperate griefs and strident symmetries,
Maimed by concussive will — as all that lives
Sustains through whole con-fusion.   Nothing pure
Can cope with time, unbrazed to the impure —
Look for no perfect art except in death.

Song Aspires to Silence

Song aspires to silence.
Men of defiant words
Look to the breaking moment
When blood will shed the fever,

Freed of the ceaseless striving
To fasten mountains and seas
And tame the resistless wills
Of hell and heaven defiant.

Song aspires to silence:
The fear that drones above
The rapt fury of song
Seeks its calm in driving

The blood to bury in words
The ever-unnameable love
That plunders the mind and
        storms the bewildered heart.

Sea Story

Two men fell in the Irish Sea
And when they had drowned they began to think.
The first said *Water is eyes, all eyes.*
And he shook off his flesh to become pure sight
Till his body changed into waves of light.

But the other, blinded, began to drink
The sea with his ears: *It is sound, pure sound:*
Listen, listen, and we'll be free
Of our eyes at last.

                    Though he wasn't heard,
He awaited the first man's answering word;
And when there came no friendly sound,
The veins of his mind swelled into rage
Till the voice of his will, too sharp to bear,
Craved release into plangent air . . .

Two men fell in the Irish Sea
And when they awoke above, they could claim
To each other the truths they had found below.
It is light, said one — and *light is death,*
He thought.   Thought the other: *And so is sound* —
But he said *There is nothing below for eyes:*
We must listen to water.

                    With brazen breath
They could argue, parry, and fume and blame,
Safe on land where they could not think,
Drowned in more than hearing or sight

And twisted by dream.   The two who fell
In the sea would fight the appeals of air
Blowing against their minds until
They could learn to balance in one calm thought
The winds of waking, the waters of sleep.

Random Pieces of a Man

Disown the face deciphered from the book:
No one but you could draw it from the mazes
Of selves wandering undisguised beneath
A line, a twist of sound.   Because the phrases

Suppress as much as they avow, denying
More than a sound's signal, what you see
Might be proclaimed of any man who speaks
Only what can be spoken faithfully

Without danger, pacing his heart's edges,
Safe from its fire core.   He has no names
To hold such heat; everything held in words
Is lava cooled: you read the ash of flames

And only such as he placed upon the page
For you to see, chosen from all his pure
And grave designs.   Where did you hope to trace
His inexpressibles of love and fear

And grief, the laughter seized and lost, the pain
Denied its song?   Though some of him is here,
The missing stares unguessable — while you,
Guarding the profile, lovingly secure

The random pieces of his time tumbled
Luckily on a page. — Oh, hold him close!
Uncertain alien, once: to you no longer
Strange.   Alas, a pattern: calm, morose,

Fretful, and other adjectives that stamp
A new cliché. — Now that you see him bare,
Will you still prize him?   His addiction (verse)
Scarcely captivates.   How could it compare

With any colorful frenzy? — Come confess:
He lacks élan . . . — If all I say is true,
Why do you scorn my words, unless the face
Deciphered from the book is chiefly you?

Innocence

In desperate dream of sleep a man
May accuse innocence.   Fearing the will
Of ardors everywhere, he can charge
Rays of the sun with kissing your face,
Accuse the wind of fondling your hair,
Rage that the air you breathe rushes
Tremblingly to touch your lips
And the silks draping your bosom and arms
Cling like hands to the moons of your breast . . .

Wading in desperate dream asleep
Or awake a man may make of heedless
Chimes a glow of beckoning truth,
Grieve to watch their burden shred
Past his reach into gatherless air:

Is sight thereafter pain-compelled
To look for the lost in a blazing world?
Drawn by trust to the trace in his eyes,
Must he believe it will one day grow
A force to quicken the corpse of dream?

In a Museum

Walk inside: don't be afraid.   The shapes
Of tender rock won't leap at you.   If they do,
You will have asked them to.   And if you bleed,
Blame the skin that presses itself to bruise
Against an edge that is sharp to the eyes only.

If any painting jeer at you from the wall,
Turn your back, blot it out with denial.
Nothing lives for you in this mute assemblage
Unless your willed consent makes it a creature
Dropped from nowhere, added upon your landscape —
Your own familiar — where it can stay or vanish
By your acknowledgement . . . like all that waits
Around you: here, outside, and anywhere:

Shapes that are lives suspended, till your sight
Summons figures out of a rigid landscape,
Troubles them with awareness.   Yours or theirs — ?
You need not stop to learn who gives the challenge

Outside or in this house.   You need not ask
Whether the faces pulsate out of a block
Of ravished stone or wear a breathy skin:
Enough: the faces live, when nothing lives
For you until its image stirs the striving
Waves of your inner sea upon whose tides
You voyage, cradled, to alert the world.

(For Leda)

Event in a Field

When the small lips of rain
Ceaselessly press at the flesh of ground,
When the gold rods of sun
Plunge in heat through the creviced grains:
However its arms resist, —
Though it bristle a skin of bitter clay
And draw in its bones from the rods of fire —
If growth once fibered its strength, land
Must give up its will to the will of air
And haven a womb for flowers.

More than a hope: this waste of clay
Unlocked from its eyeless stare, now reveling
Under a rollicking foam of daisies,
Buttercup, Indian paintbrush, green . . .

More than a thought: when stones exhale
Lakes of moaning color flaming
Leaves raveling wind.

More than vision: a sign —
The possible hung clear
Above our copeless chasm of land and sky,
To burn through the mists of a mind
When will wavers, fearing the rescue of tears.

Outcast of the Waters

No man has seen the wind, though he has heard
Always since he was young a faceless flow
Of moaning from the blue enormous bird;
But only the wind's touch could make him know,

As only the green's prevalence could prove
The tides of birth that slake the loving ground
To sight too slow to see a tendril move
And ears that never range the growing sound:

Young outcast of the waters, still unsure —
Fathered on land but mothered in a sea
Whose terrible bright naked shadows lure
In lovely lust that will not let him free:

How can he hope to gather from her wave
More than a dye dissolved in light, to find
The substance of the shape, unless he brave
Her wraith of bodies burning in his mind?

Woodpecker

Woodpecker hovering out of the dawn,
Weaving through arches of sleeping leaves,
Why do you pass the living boughs
To strike at my cabin's eaves?

To find a sweet like the sweet you draw
From the poplars, take your drills of fire
Out of these sapless hemlock halves
Shaped to a man's desire.

And since with nail and beam we have made
A mystic leafless tree you must go
For food to the files of green-leaved boughs
Where the live rootsaps flow:

Know that whatever nourishment moves
In our tree we save for a time bereaved
When age must feed itself on truth
The will of youth believed.

Tomtom of the Heartbeat

Though sung with fierce belief
And lit with crystal day,
The songs the young men sang
Our hearts now cast away.

Flesh they had fever-chilled
Creeping through time has shed
The tissues of young manhood:
Our blood has changed its red.

So must our tongue contemn them,
Our brain resist belief
Ever it bloomed to music poured
From those childish shells of grief.

We in our iron day,
Duped by caress, alone
Trust the clean, fierce burden
The fist can wring from stone.

Yet from such hollow cadence
Our will would hazard change,
And our heart, fed on a ruthless song,
Thirst for a farther range —

For the grace notes of a fugue
Where the budless mind can pore
On a plagal cadence of hope
That could justify its war:

Pale mind that beats to a music
Scored for its coward age:
A tomtom of the heartbeat
In a key of frozen rage.

Wave

No man can live on truth
Found from the rays of light,
But he must mix with truth a dream
Of truth outranging sight.

Nor can he live believing
Part of the earth his own:
Nothing of earth can be possessed.
All you have craved or won —

Tower, face, and mountain,
Wisdom, word, and tree
Ride the corroding wave that drops
All in a hollow sea.

Even the graceless ground
Where your dead loved one lies —
The wave will split apart the vault,
Thoughtless of sacrifice,

And crack the brazen shroud,
Seize the pale skin and bones
And gnaw them into dust
And feed them to the stones.

Anchorage in Time (I)

On pavements wet with the misty wind of spring
We walk while our bodies burn
For places where hands of trees draw sleep from a brook
And the air is damp with fern . . .

If waters image cloud, a man can see
A heaven underneath, but if he change
To look up at the sky, let him remember
His anchorage to earth.   Whoever stares
May see suddenly over blue pools of sky
Moving foam of cloud: at once his mind
Will fever for truth, for his anchorage in time,
Balancing earth and heaven in his eyes . . .
Then wakes from staring and puts back the sea
And sun in place, yet never again certain
Which eyes to trust, saying in voiceless words:

What is a man, who strides against the light:
A coat of flesh drawn on the bracing bones?
And the furled earth beneath his feet: a skin
Of sand muffling the burning ribs of stone?
Or is his blood an impulse of all breath:
Flesh fused with bone in one vast atomy
With sand and stone — with earth, whose ground and fire
Speaks for all breath?   Which eyes to trust, which eyes? . . .

Let those who search look to their anchorage
In time, before they balance earth and heaven.

Anchorage in Time (II)

The vast stone trunk of mountain lifts above
The ground no more nor less than its rocky knees
Have sunk in tight brown earth, while everywhere
Water is steadily grinding down the hills;
Water will pour the powder into the sea
Until the day the suns no longer boil
The air or scorch the grass,
Blowing from the pale disc of yellow stone
Not flame enough to melt the frozen wave
Blinding the rock and sea —
Hot earth become ice-star.

Yet must the mind woven of blood believe
An imaged vision scaled to an anchorage
In time, and watch eternities emerge
Out of the baseless dust: eternal spring
Conferred on land where cubicles of flesh
And thought must name themselves safe from the ardor
That walls apart all striving unities;
Admit no future fiercer than this river
Raging over cascades of ice the winter
Sun will soon take down.

The mind believes as much
As blood believes, nor grieves for surer purpose
In the immense star-endless curl of space
Than sea's or hill's or frail ephemeras'
Of air, but takes the earth and sun for truth
Eternal in a treasured now, and love
Its anchorage in time.

To a Young Girl Sleeping

Into this room of sleep let fall
    The moon's dimmest bars —
Glitter might rouse her still hands lying
    Paler than water-stars;

And let the nightwind calmly flow,
    Lay but the frailest words
On her whose face is a shadow softer
    Than evening birds'.

The Hollow River

(December 19, 1938 – January 11, 1940)

Speak these lines that no one will understand
Except the friends who know; and they must turn
From listening.   Memory-mind survives
By sure decay; a thinking grief that fattens
Kills the host.   Speak of the child who lived,
Strove for breath, fainted and laughed, cried
And sang, and died and lived a thousand hours
Through one wild-fated year, until the morning,
Babbling her song, she suddenly ceased breathing,
And sank in her mother's arms.   I write these lines
Against my hand, contemptuous of the pen,
Fighting the filthy gush of words that chokes
Until the brutal deed of verse is finished.
Kaleidoscope of drowning man asks nothing
Of floods before the bleeding eyes swell up
And close.   The books will dry, the tongue blacken,
The rib cage swell, the heart burst in the sea.

— Walking once in a thicket, I tripped on a pebble
And headlong fell on bedded vines, and suddenly
Saw a river growing out of darknesses
Choked with vining trees and bushes and arched
With thistles and wild roses.   Overhead
I saw no sky, but everywhere were drops
Of light: blue petals of the sky, white petals

Of cloud foam, red-gold petals of the sun.
I heard the light there make a heavenly sound;
The rainbow water tasted of heaven dew . . .

The smug disdain of art can compensate
For sense with quick imaginings.   Dear art,
Swooning in contemplation of the joy
You trick out of the wreckage of your love:
Deny your mummied sweetness owes its substance
To the soft corpse of fact you cover over.
— But look! weeds are pushing up from that flesh . . .
O cold, sick counterfeit of song, of a world
That dangles nowhere in the brain, lacking
Anchorage of time or space — dear travesty
Of verse to elegize this heart whose sounds
Were tiny waterfalls that brightened air —
O fragment songs of my sunbird . . .

Whoever loved the earth as a beloved,
He was a friend and comrade.   I could ask
Wanderers why they searched the world for a friend
When they could find each other as they watched
The same tree bend, the same green rainwind blow.
Now that the sickness hangs on me, I see
In every sunset the hideous chemistries
Of earth, the murder fires of transmutation
That build the color glories.   And I see
My own mirage: a box of ashes holding
The transmutation of my sunbird's song.

— The lights of earth are sinking; a great face
Breathes fires through my head; soon may come
The killing kiss, the hated eyes.

— Walking once in a thicket, I tripped on a rock-fault
And fell head-first against the matted screens
Of vine stalk.   When I wiped my eyes I could see
The grave of a river: parched and hard, with nothing
Growing out of its gray skin.   I poured water
Into the bed, I diverted the spring rains
And channeled the heavy autumn flood.   I saw
The gray skin dry up the water, then I heard
A wind coughing out of the hollow river . . .

I used to say the mad were free; we said,
We red-beaked idiot parrots, only madmen
Choose the door from truth.   And are the laws
Of madness purer or are they the same?
Try on the codes!   Is there a hole for the head?
What of your legs?   Does it cover up your eyes
Or must they close?   We have mismade our hearts.
We say the law is true, knowing it lies.
— Turn the tables.   Prepare for another law.
The world clings to its sanities by a thread
Of covenanted make-believe.   The world
.Continues sane for liars who are mad.
I break the thread, deny that goodness, justice,
Mercy, et al. — Call up the station, Heine!
Here is my piece of string not Cleopatra's
But the covenant thread from the gut of a mother of god.

—They question me.   They pry into corners,
Looking for papers with pieces of thought scribbled.
There were no words.   The songs of paradise
Were few, for paradise could use no song.
I build a house on the grave of a hollow river.
The walls are hung with pain; we brush our arms
Against them, and we look out through the panes.
The light that filters through shakes with fear.

I put my house in order; purge my head;
Open the veins of the wrist for the blood-letting;
Blow the pipes clean and let the liquid out;
Close down the windows; pull the springless blinds;
Whatever air, let stay there; shut up the house;
Make it a grave for the wind; lock up the door
Of the brain; throw the key in the well whose depths
Are dry with the homing waters of the thousand
Thousand hollow rivers of men.

November 1940

ANONYMOUS ALBA

En un vergier soiz folha d'albespi

Sheltered beneath white hawthorn boughs,
A woman held her loved one close
In her arms, till the watchman cried abroad:
God! It is dawn! How soon it's come!

"How wildly have I wished that the night
Would never end, and that my love
Could stay, and the watchman never cry
God! It is dawn! How soon it's come!

"My love-and-friend, but one more kiss,
Here in our field where the small birds sing;
We shall defy their jealous throats —
God! It is dawn! How soon it's come!

"Still one more close embrace, my love,
Here in our field where the small birds sing,
Till the watchman blow his reedy strain —
God! It is dawn! How soon it's come!

"From the wind beyond where my love has gone,
Thoughtful, contented, I have drunk
A long deep draught of his breath — O God,
God! It is dawn! How soon it's come!"

(ENVOI)

Flowing with grace and charm is she;
Her loveliness draws many eyes,
Whose full heart throbs with a true love:
God! It is dawn! How soon it's come!

Le temps a laissié ...

The weather's cast away its cloak
Of wind and rain and chilling haze;
It wears instead embroideries
Of crystal sunlit rays.

There's not a beast or bird but sings
Or calls out in his own sweet strain:
The weather's cast away its cloak
Of wind and cold and rain.

The whole wide earth is clothed anew:
River, fountain, and brook now wear
Drops of silver, frets of gold:
The weather's cast away its cloak
Of wind and rain and cold.

ANDRÉ SPIRE

Un parfum éternel ...

Smoke from heaps of turnip top
Rises, bends, and lowers
Toward the milky mists now floating
Among the furrowed clods.

Behind their steaming horses
Gigantic peasant forms,
Ploughing the muddy earth,
Labor as on a sea.

Suddenly: twigs glisten.
The leaves change into mirrors:
Heaven lives!   I possess a shadow.
The silence breaks in tatters.

My boots are light as air —
Blue rains down everywhere.

From the sea of clover blossoms
An eternal perfume rises:
My dog dives in this sea,
Then he looks at me, stretches his legs,
And his jaws chew at the wind.

He stops and I go forward
And a pheasant flies off in a cry.

ANDRÉ SPIRE

Nativité

> *Knowest thou the time when
> the wild goats of the rock
> bring forth? Or canst thou
> mark when the hinds do
> calve? They bring forth their
> young and they are delivered
> of their sorrows.*
>
> — JOB

The cat lies on her back,
Tender eyed, open mouthed,
Pale curved tongue rose-tipped . . .

The cat gasps in the night . . .
A star in the midst of branches
Gleams cold, like the rings
Of a glow-worm moving through leaves.

Now tiny heads and paws swarm
On the cat's belly softly warm.

No wind.   A leaf falls.

ANDRÉ SPIRE

Nudités

Hair is a nudity. — THE TALMUD

You said to me:
I would become your comrade:
I would visit your house without fear of troubling you.
We shall spend evenings in talk together,
Talking and thinking of our murdered brothers;
Together we shall wander the earth to find
A country to quiet their heads at last.
But do not let me see your eyeballs glitter
Or the burning veins of your forehead bulge!
I am your equal, not a prey.
Look at me: my clothes are chaste, almost poor!
You cannot even see the curve of my throat!

I looked and I answered:
Woman, you are naked:
Your downy neck is a goblet of well-water,
Your locks are wanton as a troop of mountain goats,
Your round, soft chignon quivers like a breast —
Woman, cut off your hair!

You are naked: your hands now lie unfurled,
Open in nakedness across the printed page,
Your fingers, the subtle tips of your body,
Ringless fingers — that will touch mine any moment —
Woman, cut off your hands!

You are naked: your voice flows up from your bosom,
Your song, your breath, and now the heat of your flesh —
It is spreading round my body to enter my flesh —
Woman, tear out your voice!

ANDRÉ SPIRE

Ce n'est pas toi . . .

It was not you I was waiting for
Since the beginning, always.
It was not you I saw in my dreams —
Boyhood dreams, young man's dreams.
It was not you I searched for
In the pretty bodies I loved,
Nor was it you I watched descending
The hills in a blaze of light.
— We were going our separate ways,
Our paths suddenly crossed
And we held out our hands to each other.

The days have fled,
My beloved one . . .

from

THE IRON LAND

(1936)

It is rarely that the wind alone can move large stones.
— WATTS (GEOLOGY FOR BEGINNERS)

Bread

This that I give you now,
This bread that your mouth receives,
Never knows that its essence
Slept in the hanging leaves

Of a waving wheatfield thriving
With the sun's light, soil, and the rain,
A season ago, before knives
And wheels took life from the grain

That leaf might be flour — and the flour
Bread for the breathers' need . . .
Nor cared that some night one breather
Might watch how each remnant seed

Invades the blood, to become
Your tissue of flesh, and molests
Your body's secrets, swift-changing
To arms and the mounds of your breasts,

To thigh, hand, hair, to voices,
Your heart and your woman's mind . . .
For whatever the bread, do not grieve now
That soon a flash of the wind

May hurry away what remains
Of this quiet valiance of grass:
It entered your body, it fed you
So that you too can pass

From valiance to quiet, from thriving
To silenced flesh, and to ground:
Such is our meager cycle
That turns but a single round

For the deathless flesh of the earth,
For the signless husks of men dead,
For the folded oceans and mountains,
For birds, and fields, and for bread.

End of the Flower-World

Fear no longer for the lone gray birds
That fall beneath the world's last autumn sky,
Mourn no more the death of grass and tree.

These will be as they have ever been:
Substance of springtime; and when flower-world ends,
They will go back to earth, and wait, and be still,

Safe with the dust of birds long dead, with boughs
Turned ashes long ago, that still are straining
To leave their tombs and find the hills again,

Flourish again, mindless of the people —
The strange ones now on a leafless earth
Who seem to have no care for things in blossom.

Fear no more for trees, but mourn instead
The children of these strange, sad men: their hearts
Will hear no music but the song of death.

Willowy Wind

Now let us two lie down in willowy wind
And raise eyes upward upon pale cloud
And watch birds flutter soft-weaving wings;

See pale cloud-drift float and idle by
To melt in the windy waters of the sky . . .
Gaze only above us, nor wonder why.

Then turning eyes inward, remembering cloud,
Hope that our bodies be taken into the stream
Of wind, and wish our blood a willowy dream.

Days

Strange to be torn away from your embrace
  In the cold dawn,
To be taken far from your face, your silence,
  To be drawn

Past streets, fields, rivers, toward a place
  Miles, miles away
Where senseless words and images clog the mind
  Till the end of day,

When, turning back to you, I wonder, moving
  Through twilight haze,
If we must live only in meeting and parting
  The rest of our days.

A Coil of Glass (I)

Somewhere there is a coil of glass within
Whose range the fire of stars
Thousands of light-years gone gives back the gleam
Once shed from earth —
Lost light of crumpled hours.

He who finds this glass
Reclaims at will whatever sleeps in time.
Nothing that was need ever fade so long
As air floods the redoubts of space and worlds
Roll on their pivots:
All the dead years sleep
On the faces of quiet stars.

Whoever owns this glass may one day turn
The lenses toward the face
Of the farthest star and bring at last a sight
For which men grieved through lightless
Centuries: first moment
A seed of dust unloosed the multiple flowers
Bound in its atom strength, and locked the shapes
In one vast whole of interbalanced need,
And broke forever the vile or sacred sound
Of earth before men quarreled with the ground.

A Coil of Glass (II)

A book might be the lens of pure hard tears,
The coil of glass that sights whatever sleeps
In time — gone light of earth holding the crumpled hours.
Focus the glass at will: look at the man —
Adam, Arthur, Christ.   Look at the woman —
Lilith, Iseult, Helen.   Light up the brain
Of the priests and kings, the file
Of heroes set on the seeded steps of time.
Then watch these idols crash on the floor of your mind.

Mythless your heart breaks
On the edges of days revived.   Nothing can heal
The wound until you learn the lens, until you know
Builders of myth were men whose hungering minds,
Cutting through shells of sense, needed to image
The fact they hoped to see.

Focus the glass at will: it may show how men
First rose up, lost in the jungle's day
And found themselves in the dim fraternities of blood-and-
    mind,
Only to lose themselves again in a darker
Fiercer jungle, where wind
Is scissored by screams from a lightless ground,
Where feet trample on bleeding skulls —

Our world — our father's world. . . . Our night is broken
In a coil of glass.
Look through the pure hard tears.
What do you see?
Whose hands are pushing up through the darkness?   Whose
    eyes
Carry a flame of signs that tell how the earth's
Long fierce darkness shall be plumed with suns?

Restful Ground

I have known solitudes, but none has been
Such as I seek this hour: a place so still
That the darkened grasses wake to no sound at all
Nor flutter shadowy fingers in a wind.

I have known quiet in places without dark trees,
But after this clanging of hours I seek a silence
Where the only motion is the quiet breathing
Of dark boughs gazing on the restful ground.

Waiting in Winter

They were tired, tired, and outside
The wind was cracking boughs and breaking leaves
With stones of freezing water.   Once they heard
A whistle leap and groan against the night
Like a dying bird.

Though winter-sickened, yet they tried to watch
In wonder through the window at the snow,
Content no more to feel their teardrops flow
Upon their faces as a kiss of rain,
While in their bodies gnawed the old, limp pain
Of those who live too long on love.

They were so chill, they slipt their scraggly hands
Around each other's arms. — Sleep always stills,
They thought; maybe its lie would close the day
Of two gray walkers, wordless, old, and bled
Of trust and unbelief,
Waiting in winter, withered by a sun
That fattened on their hearts and now was dead.

This War Is Love

Reverence mercy by thriving day,
Worship tenderness when the soft bloom
Of night lowers, but know that these
Are gods of doom
Leading you slowly, helpless away
To a faithless tomb.

In the dim hours of slow emergent
Hope heed the wild voice of the brave
Striving against their masters, shouting
"No words can save —
Struggle is all of blood's commandment:
This war is love."

Blood

Cats move like water,
Dogs like wind . . .
Only when bodies
Have shut out mind

Can they learn the calm
Motion of dream.

Would we could know
The way men moved
When thought was only
A great dark love

And blood lay calm
In a depthless dream.

For a Workers' Road-Song

Strange that this ripple of birds we hear
Has always sung in the May of the year
Over the road where thousands pass
In the warm ripe wind that lifts from grass,

But stranger that we should have a thought
For a bird or the smell that a branch has brought,
Who give our strength at a wheel that yields
Each day new weapons to ruin fields.

Notes

p. 26, penultimate line: Genesis I: 28-30.

p. 40: lines 6–8: Amir Gilboa, contemporary poet, in *The Modern Hebrew Poem Itself*, Stanley Burnshaw, T. Carmi, Ezra Spicehandler, editors; Schocken (paperback), pp. 136*f*.

p. 49: The Rock (*hatsúr*) is one of the Hebrew appellations of God.

p. 50: see Jerry McGahan, "The Condor. . . " in the *National Geographic*, May 1971.

p. 54: Verweile doch, Du bist so schön: the words appear twice in Goethe's *Faust*, with slightly differing punctuation (Part I, Act I, line 1700; Part II, Act V, line 11580). Walter Kaufmann renders the former: *"Werd ich zum Augenblicke sagen:/ Verweile doch! Du bist so schön!"* as "If to the moment I should say:/ Abide, you are so fair."

p. 59: The poem presents Mallarmé's quest: the seven scenes follow a career from the opening "Dedication" to the "Waking" out of the dream that it was: of abstracting from the world of sensation the essences that are the truth, truth of a special sort. In I, the first scene, he dedicates himself to this searching act: not only to find what these essences are but to create, after finding them, by naming them. "So to compose the universe," by decomposing it into its essences and then by the remaking of them into the "Orphic Book of the Earth," which (as he considered it) was the collaborative effort of all poets. Once found, these essences can create a universe of their own, a new "eternity of words." And so he goes forth, confronting the sensate world with the belief that "Even flesh can be burned/ To the whitenesses of a song."

pp. 60f: A teacher by profession, he goes to his classroom for his daily work—but worried by the insignificance of what he is teaching in the light of his quest. He dreams of brushing aside the textbooks and lessons to tell the students the great truth that he knows and is also seeking. How? He thinks of saying this to his students: that a mirror transforms the object it reflects into its abstract self, its truth.—And then he comes to feel it would be hopeless to try to persuade them to his thought: "Open your pages! Safer to eye a book!" But one of the students refuses—and suddenly he (Mallarmé) has become a mirror into which the boy gazes. Confused by what has happened to his own sentient self, he nevertheless knows that he has become a mirror gazing back into the boy and drawing out of this human object the essences that "mirrors" are able to draw out of the sensate world that they take in. And so he asks himself the terrible question: Can he "gaze it out of substance, flesh that trembles?"

p. 62: In a later contemplation of this experience, he tries to unravel his beliefs: a soliloquy from a window, a man gazing at some flowers. The thoughts floating into his mind as he gazes suggest some of the beliefs he had uttered about essence. The quotation I have kept in French in the Notes is difficult to put into English, but it contains the thought of this scene—he is seeking from the flowers the essential flowerness, that which is "absent from all bouquets." To be found, it must be removed (from all bouquets), leaving only the idea of flower. "Where have you gone, my petals?" he asks as by his force of mind he removes their presences. "Go to return, vanish as you return," he commands them now, but the second "return" is a return by living. Hence when they return to him they will not be flowers he can touch or smell but the essence-idea that will "live in a thrust of mind."

p. 63: The experience stays with him as he looks elsewhere on the sensate world—"Not only petals," he says. His other self answers: "Whatever waits" can stare back at the gazer to make itself known (a parallel of a kind to what happened in II, when the boy gazed back at the teacher). The scene continues in dialogue to its conclusive thoughts—that what comes out of this staring, which is a burning (I: "Even flesh can be burned/ To the whitenesses of a song"), is the "hovering fume"; an essence that floats in the air (recalling the suggestion of the word "spirit").

p. 64: And now, in Scene V, he is filled with a hovering fume—floating out of many different sensory objects. He speaks with words that signify absence, silence, nothingness, and in the fourth and fifth stanzas he cries out his resolution: in a Poem of Flight from sentience, he will create a song that cannot be heard by the ears of sense, for it will be pure flame—the flame out of which the fume of essence arises as pure idea...

p. 65: Even out of the experience of human flesh in its inexpressibly consuming sense—of love-embrace, immolation, self-loss. Mallarmé's obsessive fascination by blond hair becomes a river of sensuous-sensual ectasy—the "blond torrent" into which he dives and on which he asks to be borne, where he can relive "the sleeping/ Ecstasy of the ages" at once "Lost [and] found in her golden foam." And then—the final desperate act: to destroy this power of the flesh, to kill at last, to plunge into "the death/ Of love," so that he may rise up—from his finally silenced blood, no longer to be torn by the terrible forces of sense enflamed and enflaming; to rise up, holding the thing he has sought, the prize: the "ash of" the "flame" that is human life.

p. 66: He is shaken out of the dream—and the quest—for when his body answered, his "blood rebelled,/ Heart screeched at the ribs," and when he spoke the words of idea-essence (I: words that had "burned/ To the whitenesses of a song"), vision "burst." And he saw creation itself, the infinitely encompassing mirror, "gaze on itself through" him. Yet "the dream that ravaged has remade"—and he speaks with his familiar symbols through the remaining lines: of night, day, nothingness, purity. Waking into the transfigured reality from his dream (transfigured by the dream-into-waking), he cries out of the wakened quest, "O Poem/ Of Flight, abolish wings" (thus silencing the Poem of Flight invoked in V, which bore his hope). The concluding lines of this scene are the confession of what I have put in the Note: "Mon art est un impasse" (with its reverberating suggestions, which also pervade) "Ici-bas est maître." And so: the final line.

pp. 71–80: For their generous help with one or more of these Second-Hand Poems, I record my warm gratitude to Frederic Ernst, the late Dudley Fitts, Elena Levin, Solita Soledad Marichal, Octavio Paz, Henri Peyre, Paul P. Rogers, and Mme André Spire. Titles: p. 70 "Beyond Love"; p. 73, "The Swifts' Return"; p. 74, "The Deceiving Angel"; p. 75, "Song of the Unlucky Angel"; p. 76, "The Spade."

p. 83: For readers who suspect that a writer writes only one book regardless of the number of volumes he may compose, this paragraph from my "Three Revolutions of Modern Poetry": "The war was, of course, inevitable, man being what he is: a maker of tools and bent on mastery. Actually he had always been moving toward an open declaration, from the ancient moment when he developed the hand axe and the flint in his struggle for food and survival. The intervening preparatory stages can be traced by anyone who studies the evolution of science and technology down through what we call the Age of Reason. By that time, of course, the intellectual elite of England had ceased to be intimidated by the forces of Nature. Nature was less a mystery than a machine. But it was not until animal power had been displaced by waterpower and steampower that the war began in earnest. From that point on it was simply a question of time, one thing leading to another until the discovery and use of atomic power. The war against Nature had been confidently waged and won; and we post-moderns, of 1945-and-after, breathe the spirit of a different epoch, and we have a different terror on our minds: Now that man is victorious, how shall he stay alive?" (*Varieties of Literary Experience,* New York, 1962, p. 138.)

p. 90, lines 13–17: "The Story of the Shipwrecked Sailor," in Adolf Erman, *Literature of the Ancient Egyptians,* London, 1927, p. 30.

p. 103: the blooming buzzing confusion—William James's phrase, *Principles of Psychology,* 1890, vol. 1, p. 488.

p. 118: Readers familiar with the *Dayenu* passage of the Passover service may see the debt of this poem to the form of that responsive reading ("If He had not drowned our oppressors in the Red Sea/ But had delivered us upon dry land/ It would have been sufficient"). At the time this particular house was occupied, Jews were officially denied the right to live in that city. Third stanza from last: "Home"=Zion.

p. 135: perhaps a third-hand, rather than second-hand, poem: translated from the French of Sophie Laffitte, *Anna Akhmatova: Poésies,* Paris, 1959.

p. 136, line 6: the final word (*Wesen*) means "creature," "essence," "being," "condition," "existence," etc. The final word of the poem (*Dinge*) means not only "things" but also "beings," "creatures," "objects," etc.

p. 137, line 10: *Font s'évaporer les soleils.*

p. 140: Omitted from line 13: [*Ton linge brûlant ta peau*] *comme le foyer d'une lentille.* The final line is *Connais, connais ton Dieu!*

p. 141: Translated with the help of Solita Soledad Marichal. The final word (*estancia*) means "room," "dwelling," "stay," etc.

p. 145, line 18: *The private man's infinitude defies.* "In all my lectures I have taught one doctrine, namely, the infinitude of the private man." —Emerson, in his *Diary,* 1840.

p. 146, line 3: *Parsons,* one of the seven workmen sentenced to death in the Haymarket Square incident, Chicago, 1886.

p. 147, line 15: "Respondez!" first published (1856) as "Poem of the Proposition of Nakedness"; as No. 5, "Chants Democratic," in 1860; as "Respondez!" in 1867, 1870. In his broadside "The Eighteenth Presidency" (written in 1856), Whitman wrote: "What historic dé-nouements are these we are approaching? On all sides tyrants tremble, crowns are unsteady, the human race is restive, on watch for some better era, some divine war." In his preface to a British edition of *Specimen Days,* Whitman emphasized as the "basic phrase" of all his writings: "Good-will between the common people of all nations." "A new and tender reverence" are also Whitman's words.

p. 147, line 27: "Everything that can be believ'd is an image of truth." Blake, *Marriage of Heaven and Hell.*

p. 148, lines 8–10: Horace Traubel reports Whitman's statement: "That is the same old question—adjusting the individual to the mass. Yes, the big problem, the only problem: the sum of them all."

p. 183: last lines, *cf.* p. 126, lines 10*f.*